walkermaths 2.14

SYSTEMS OF EQUATIONS

NCEA Level 2 Internal

Charlotte Walker and Victoria Walker

Walker Maths 2.14 Systems of Equations
1st Edition
Charlotte Walker
Victoria Walker

Designer: Cheryl Smith, Macarn Design
Production controller: Siew Han Ong

Acknowledgements
Cover photo courtesy of Shutterstock.

We wish to thank the Boards of Trustees of Darfield and Riccarton High Schools for allowing us to use materials and ideas developed while teaching. Our thanks also go to all past and present colleagues who have generously shared their experience and ideas.

For product information and technology assistance,
in Australia call **1300 790 853**;
in New Zealand call **0800 449 725**

For permission to use material from this text or product, please email
aust.permissions@cengage.com

National Library of New Zealand Cataloguing-in-Publication Data
A catalogue record for this book is available from the National Library of New Zealand.

978 0 17 041600 9

Cengage Learning Australia
Level 7, 80 Dorcas Street
South Melbourne, Victoria Australia 3205

Cengage Learning New Zealand
Unit 4B Rosedale Office Park
331 Rosedale Road, Albany, North Shore 0632, NZ

For learning solutions, visit **cengage.co.nz**

Printed in China by 1010 Printing International Limited.
7 8 25

CONTENTS

Glossary **4**

Straight lines **5**

The gradient of a line 5
Finding the equation of a straight line 8
1 Using the gradient and the y-intercept 8
2 Using the gradient and one point 10
3 Using two points 12
4 From practical information 14
Putting it all together 16

Recognising graphs of curves **17**

Parabolas 17
Parabolas — matching equations with graphs 21
Circles 24
Circles — matching equations with graphs 27
Hyperbolas 29
Hyperbolas — matching equations with graphs 33
Mixing it up 35

Quadratic expressions **37**

Expanding 37
Factorising quadratics 39
1 Where the coefficient of x^2 is 1 39
2 Where the coefficient of x^2 is not 1, but there is a common factor 41
3 Where the coefficient of x^2 is not 1 and there is a no common factor 42
Solving quadratic equations 44
1 By factorising 44
2 Using the quadratic formula 46
3 On a calculator 48
Finding how many solutions exist 49

Simultaneous equations **52**

Line and parabola 52
Line and circle 56
Line and hyperbola 60
Finding unknown values, given the number of solutions 64
Mixing it up, with applications 68

Practice tasks **78**

Answers **85**

Glossary

Make your own glossary of key terms:

Term	Definition	Picture/Example
Parabola		
Circle		
Hyperbola		
Simultaneous		
Inequation		
Intercept		
Gradient		
Asymptote		
Coefficient		
Constant		
Linear		
Tangent		
Origin		

ISBN: 9780170416009

Straight lines

The gradient of a line

- The gradient is the steepness, or slope, of a line.
- Parallel lines have the same gradient.

These lines all have **positive** gradients.

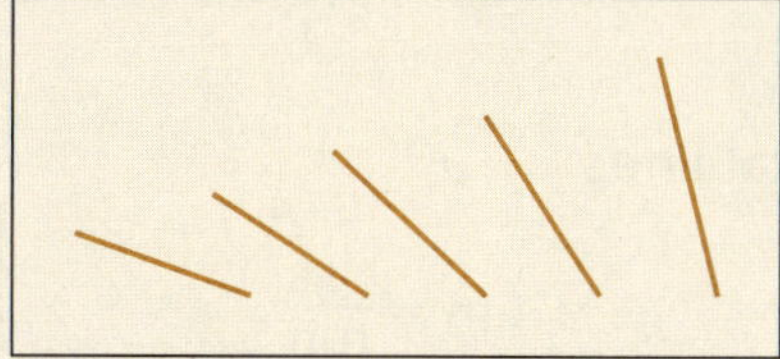

These lines all have **negative** gradients.

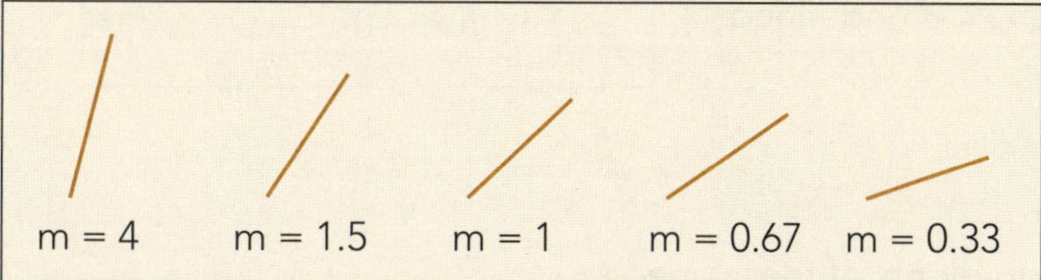

The steeper the line, the bigger the gradient.

The gradient is calculated using the formula $\mathbf{m = \frac{change\ in\ y}{change\ in\ x}}$ or $\mathbf{\frac{rise}{run}}$.

The easiest way to do this is to draw a right-angled triangle on the line.

$$m = \frac{rise}{run}$$

$$= \frac{5}{6}$$

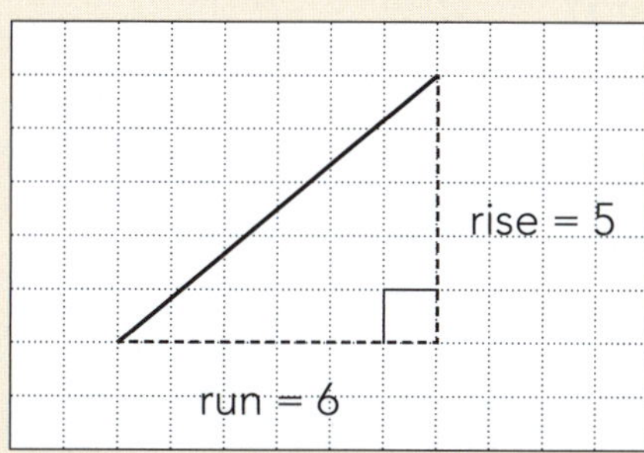

This time the gradient is **negative**.

$$m = -\frac{rise}{run}$$

$$= -\frac{3}{7}$$

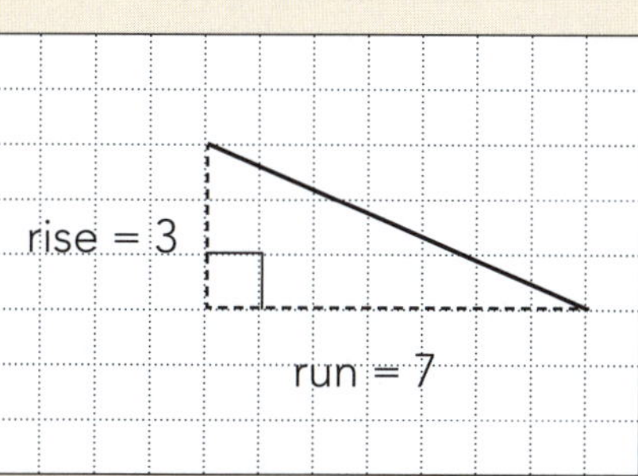

ISBN: 9780170416009

Horizontal lines

$$m = \frac{\text{rise}}{\text{run}}$$

$$= \frac{0}{7}$$

$$= 0$$

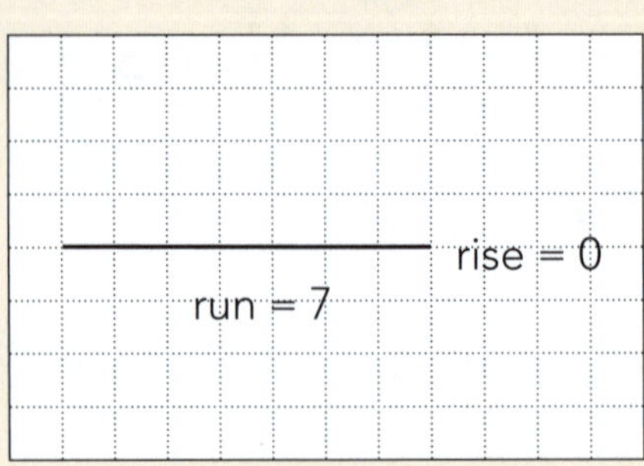

Vertical lines

$$m = \frac{\text{rise}}{\text{run}}$$

$$= \frac{5}{0}$$

$$= \text{undefined}$$

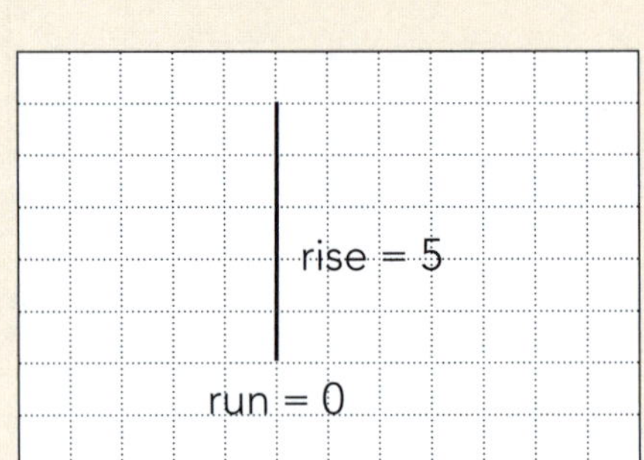

1 Calculate the gradients of these lines.

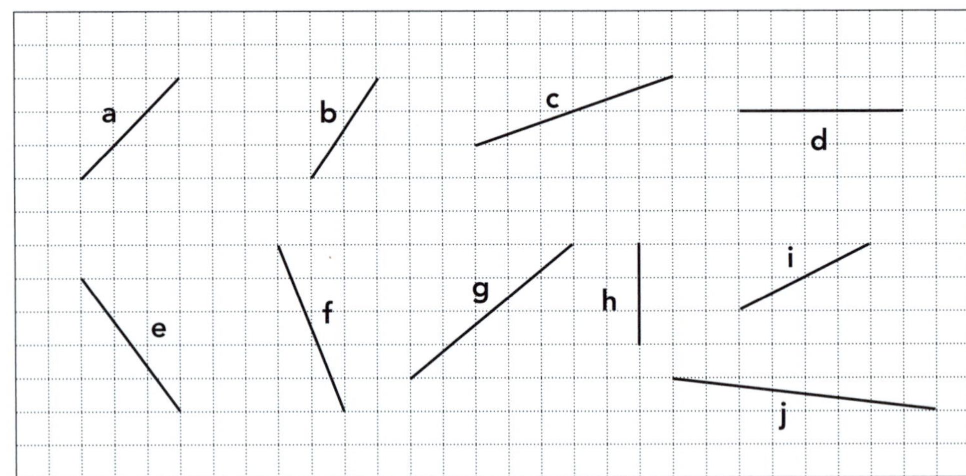

a Gradient = ______________ **b** Gradient = ______________

c Gradient = ______________ **d** Gradient = ______________

e Gradient = ______________ **f** Gradient = ______________

g Gradient = ______________ **h** Gradient = ______________

i Gradient = ______________ **j** Gradient = ______________

 ISBN: 9780170416009

2 Draw line segments to show these gradients.

a $m = \frac{1}{4}$

b $m = \frac{2}{5}$

c $m = 1$

d $m = -1$

e $m = -\frac{1}{3}$

f $m = \frac{3}{4}$

g $m = -0.6$

h $m = 1.\dot{3}$

i $m = -5$

j $m = -1.25$

Finding the equation of a straight line

This usually takes the form: **y = mx + c**

gradient = $\frac{\text{rise}}{\text{run}}$ (m)

y-intercept (c)

1 Using the gradient and the y-intercept

Example:

1 From the graph,
c = y-intercept = **–2**

2 On the line, draw a right-angled triangle anywhere to find

m = gradient = $-\frac{6}{10} = -\frac{3}{5}$

3 Substitute these into **y = mx + c**

to get: $y = -\frac{3}{5}x - 2$

m	c	y = mx + c
$-\frac{3}{5}$	–2	$y = -\frac{3}{5}x - 2$

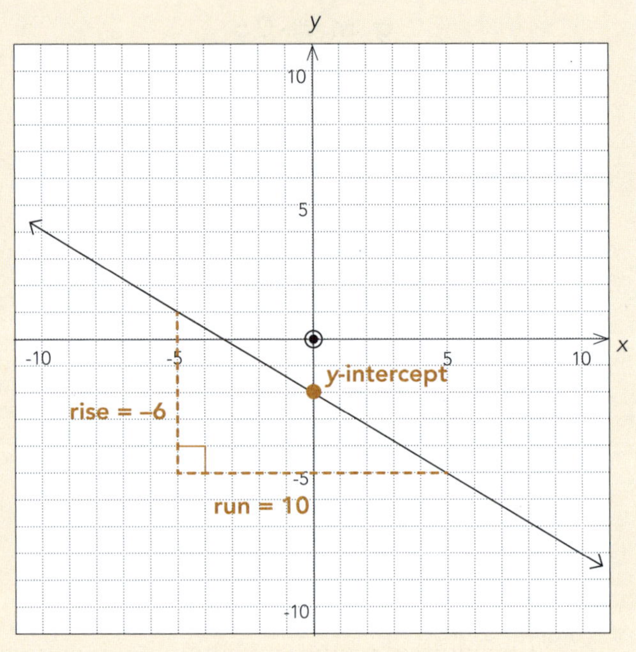

1 Complete the table.

Line	m	c	y = mx + c
———			
- - - - - -			
- - - - (orange)			
- — -			
——— (grey)			
——— (orange)			

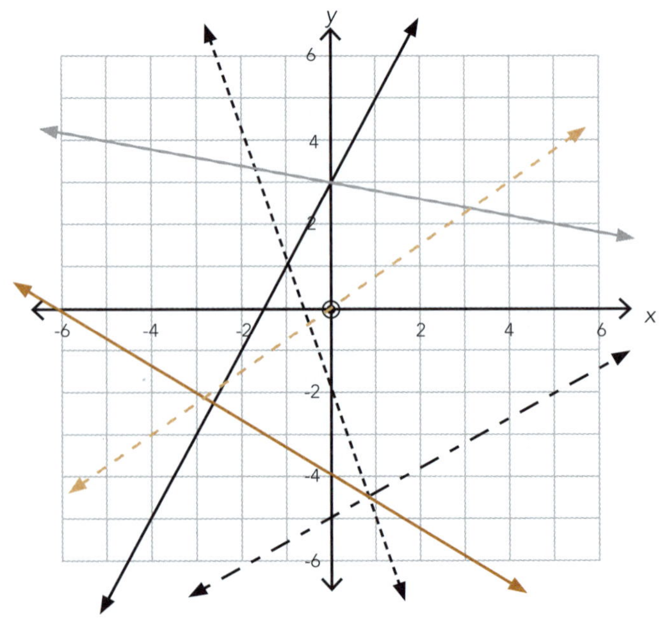

 ISBN: 9780170416009

2 Write down the equation of the line that passes through the point (0, 5) and which has a gradient of –2.

3 An equation with a gradient of 1.5 passes through the point (0, –3). Write down its equation.

4 The y-intercept of a line is 2.5, and its gradient is 0. Write down its equation.

5 A line passes through the point (0, 4) and is parallel to the line $y = 7x + 2$. Write down its equation.

6 A line passes through the origin and is parallel to the line $y = -\frac{1}{3}x - 4$. Write down its equation.

7 A line has a y-intercept of 5 and is parallel to the line $3y = 4x - 2$. Write down its equation.

8 Write down the equation of a line that passes through the point (0, –3) and is parallel to $y = px + 7$.

9 Write down the equation of a line that passes through the point (0, q) and is parallel to $y = -\frac{2}{5}x - 1$.

ISBN: 9780170416009

2 Using the gradient and one point

We use a different form of $y = mx + c$.
If the point is written (x_1, y_1), then $y - y_1 = m(x - x_1)$

Example: Find the equation of the line that has a gradient of $-\frac{1}{2}$ and which passes through the point (4, –3).

$(x_1, y_1) = (4, -3)$

$x_1 = 4$ $y_1 = -3$

$$\therefore\ y - (-3) = -\frac{1}{2}(x - 4)$$
$$y + 3 = -\frac{1}{2}x + 2$$
$$y = -\frac{1}{2}x - 1$$

Find the equation for each line using the point and gradient given.

1 (3, 4) with a gradient of 5

2 (–1, 4) with a gradient of 3

3 (4, –5) with a gradient of $\frac{1}{2}$

4 (7, 2) with a gradient of –1

5 (5, –2) with a gradient of 0

6 (0, –3) with a gradient of $-\frac{1}{2}$

 ISBN: 9780170416009

7 (8, –3) with a gradient of $\frac{3}{4}$

8 (–5, 3) with a gradient of $-\frac{5}{8}$

9 Find the equation of a line that is parallel to $y = 2x - 3$ and which passes through the point (6, 5).

10 Find the equation of a line that is parallel to $y = -\frac{2}{3}x - 7$ and which passes through the point (9, 2).

11 Find the equation of a line that is parallel to $4y = 5x - 2$ and which passes through the point (3, –11).

12 Find the equation of a line that is parallel to $3y = 7 - 4x$ and which passes through the point (0, 9).

13 Find the equation of a line which is parallel to $4y + 5 - 9x = 0$, and which passes through the origin.

3 Using two points

We use the same formula as above, but calculate the gradient first.
If the two points are $(\mathbf{x_1}, \mathbf{y_1})$ and $(\mathbf{x_2}, \mathbf{y_2})$, then:

$$\mathbf{m = \frac{y_2 - y_1}{x_2 - x_1}} \quad \text{and} \quad \mathbf{y - y_1 = m(x - x_1)}$$

Example: Find the equation of the line that passes through (4, –3) and (–6, 2).

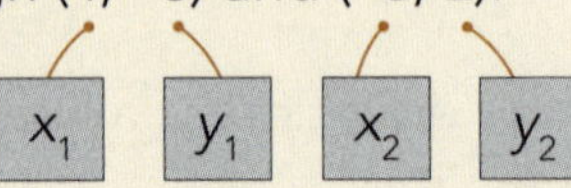

$$\therefore \; y - (-3) = \frac{2 - (-3)}{-6 - 4}(x - 4)$$

$$y + 3 = \frac{5}{-10}x + 2$$

$$y = -\frac{1}{2}x - 1$$

Calculate the equation of the line that connects the following pairs of points.

1 (0, 7) and (1 ,10)

2 (2, 8) and (1, 3)

3 (2, 5) and (6, 7)

4 (8, 3) and (4, 0)

ISBN: 9780170416009

5 (2, 1) and (6, –7)

6 (2, –9) and (4, –11)

7 (8, 2) and (0, 3)

8 (9, 2) and (–3, –6)

9 (3, 17) and (–6, 2)

10 (8, 4) and (16, –2)

11 (8, –8) and (–16, 1)

12 (5, –19) and (–20, –4)

ISBN: 9780170416009

4 From practical information

- If you need to find several values, it is usually easiest to select the smaller value as your variable.
- Often it is useful to draw a diagram.

Words used for the four basic operations:

+	plus, total, more, and, add(ed), increased by, at least, greater than, sum	–	subtract(ed), less, decreased by, smaller than
×	of, times, multiplied by, product	÷	divided by, shared between

Note: 'Double' and 'twice' both mean multiply by two.

Example 1: A group of people go to a movie. Children's tickets (x) cost \$8 and adult tickets (y) cost \$15. The total cost of the tickets was \$147.

$$8x + 15y = 147$$

Example 2: An isosceles triangle has equal sides of length x cm, and a perimeter of y.

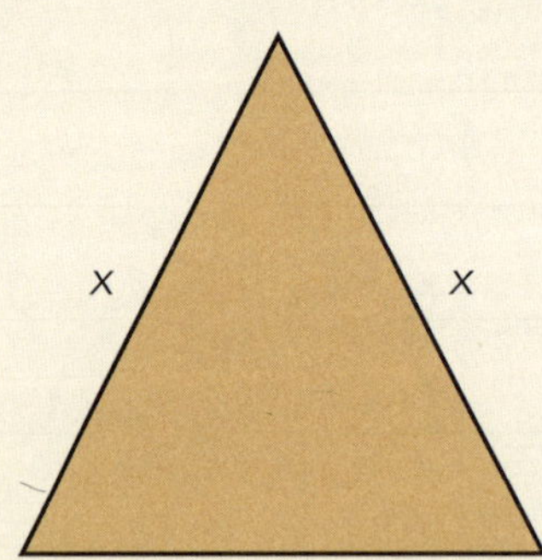

a Write an expression for the perimeter (y) if the difference between a long side (x) and a short side is 4 cm.

$$y = x + x + (x - 4)$$

$$y = 3x - 4$$

b Write an expression for the perimeter if a long side (x) is three times the length of a short side.

$$y = x + x + \frac{x}{3}$$

$$y = \frac{7x}{3}$$

 ISBN: 9780170416009

Write equations for the following situations.

1 The school produced a show. Let x represent the number of children's tickets sold, and y represent the number of adult tickets. The ticket price for children was $5, and that for adults was $12.

a On the first night, the total number of tickets sold was 258.

____

b The ticket sales on the second night totalled $2418.

____

c On the third night, 17 more children's tickets than adult tickets were sold.

____

d At a special matinee session, the number of children's tickets sold was three times the number of adult tickets sold.

____

e For the finale, if they had sold five more children's tickets, then they would have sold twice as many children's tickets as adult tickets.

____

____

f Over the entire season, the school earned $1781 more from the sale of adult tickets than from children's tickets.

____

____

2 Consider a number of rectangles. Let the longer side be x cm and the shorter side be y cm long.

a For the first rectangle, the perimeter is 84 cm.

____

b The difference between the lengths of the sides of the second rectangle is 6 cm.

____

c For the third rectangle, the longer side is 1 cm less than twice the shorter side.

____

d There are two ways to bisect a rectangle with a line that is parallel with one of its sides. Find expressions for the perimeter of the smaller rectangles that are formed in each case.

____

____

ISBN: 9780170416009

Putting it all together

Answer the following.

1 **a** The lowest point of a parabola passes through the point (5, 2).

i Write down the equation of the horizontal line that passes through this point.

ii Write down the equation for the axis of symmetry for this parabola.

b A line passes through two points on the parabola. It cuts the y-axis at (0, 3) and has a gradient of 1. Write down its equation.

c Another line cuts the parabola at (2, 11) and (7, 6). Find its equation.

d A tangent to the parabola touches it at the point (4, 3), and has a gradient of –2. Find its equation.

2 **a** A diameter of a circle passes through the point (0, 1) and has a gradient of $\frac{3}{4}$. Write down the equation of this diameter.

b A radius passes through the points (11, 3) and (8, 7). Write down the equation of this radius.

c A tangent to the circle passes through the point (4, 10), with a gradient of $\frac{4}{3}$. Find the equation of this tangent.

ISBN: 9780170416009

Recognising graphs of curves

- You do **not** need to be able to **draw** graphs of curves for this standard, although sometimes it might be useful.
- You **do** need to be able to **match** graphs of curves to their equations.
- If you do need to know what the graph looks like:
  1. Make a table
  2. Plot the points
  3. Join the points to form a smooth curve.

Parabolas

- The **parabola** is the shape of the graph obtained when any **quadratic** equation is plotted.
- A quadratic equation is an expression in which the highest power of the variable (x) is **2**.

Recognising quadratic expressions

The expanded form will **always** contain an x^2.

		Examples
Expanded form:	$y = ax^2 \pm bx \pm c$	$y = -x^2 + 5x - 2$
		$y = 0.5x^2 + 9$
		$y = -3x^2$
Factorised forms:	$y = a(x \pm d)(x \pm e)$	$y = (x - 1)(x + 6)$
		$y = -0.5(x + 7)(x - 3)$
	$y = a(x \pm f)^2 \pm g$	$y = -(x - 1)^2$
		$y = 4(x + 3)^2 - 7$
	$y = ax(x \pm j)$	$y = x(x - 1)$
		$y = 0.1x(x + 3)$

A basic parabola: $y = x^2$

x	$y = x^2$
3	9
2	4
1	1
0	0
–1	1
–2	4
–3	9

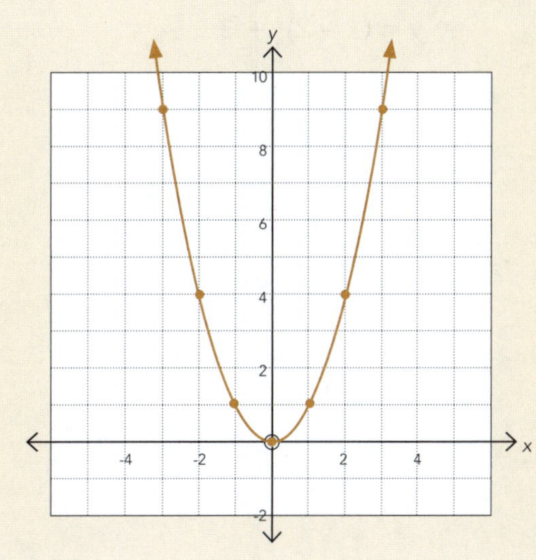

ISBN: 9780170416009

Using transformations of parabolas to find the position of the turning point

Vertical translation

$y = x^2 + 4$

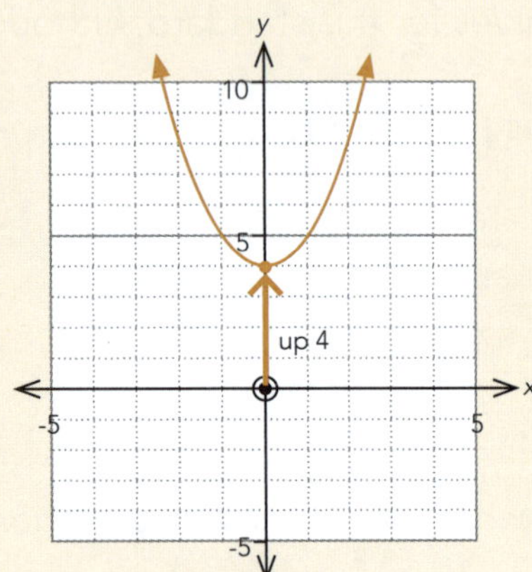

$y = x^2 - 3$

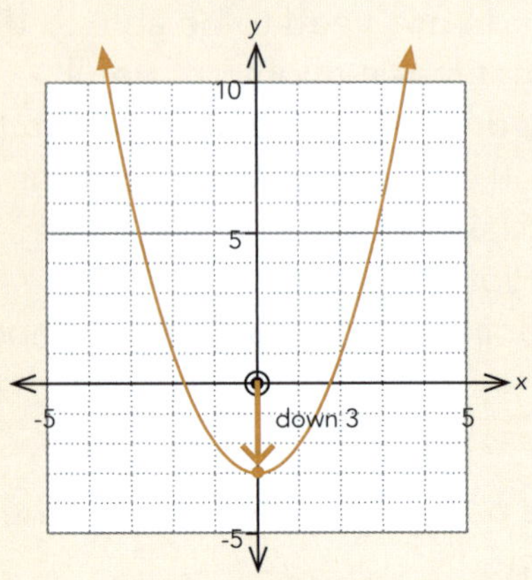

Horizontal translation

- Notice that the graph moves in the **opposite** direction to the sign.

$y = (x + 2)^2$

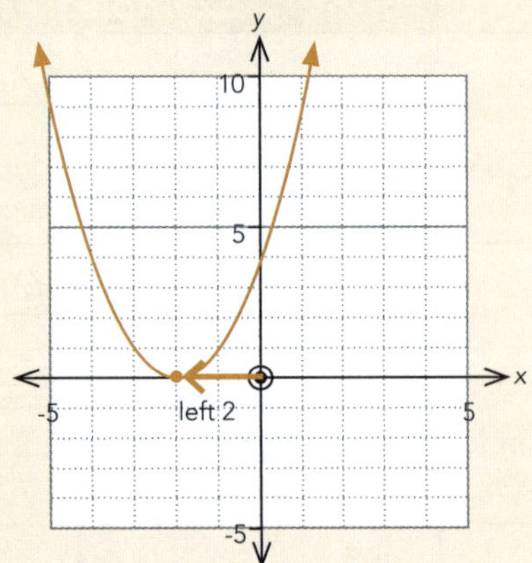

$y = (x - 3)^2$

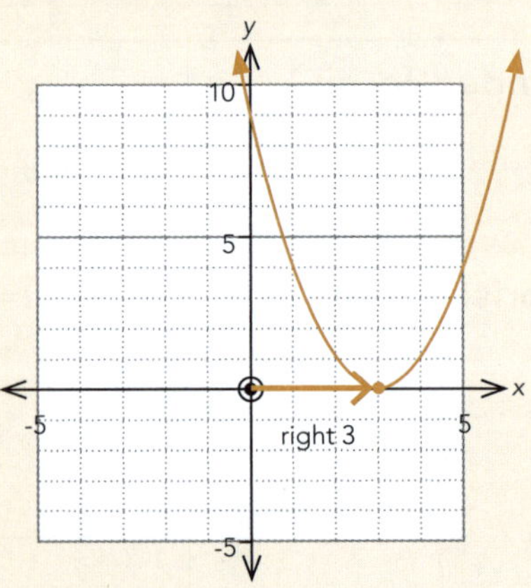

Combinations

$y = (x - 2)^2 + 3$

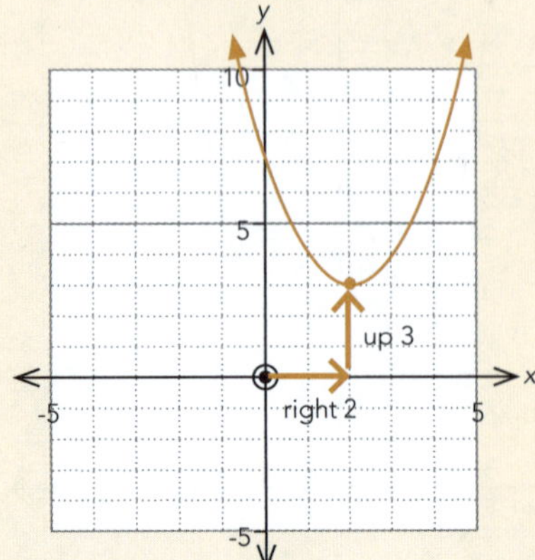

$y = (x + 3)^2 - 2$

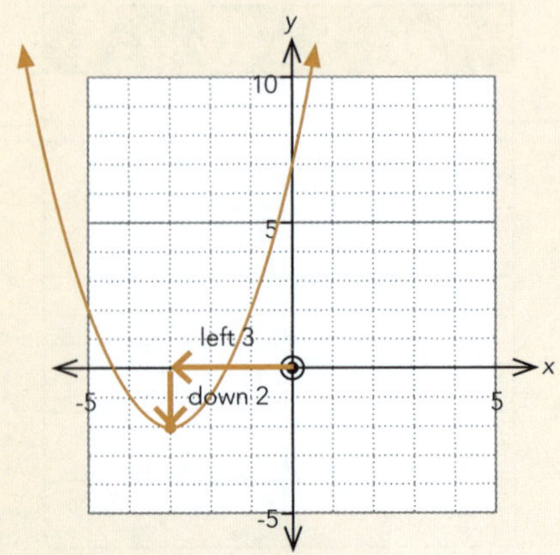

ISBN: 9780170416009

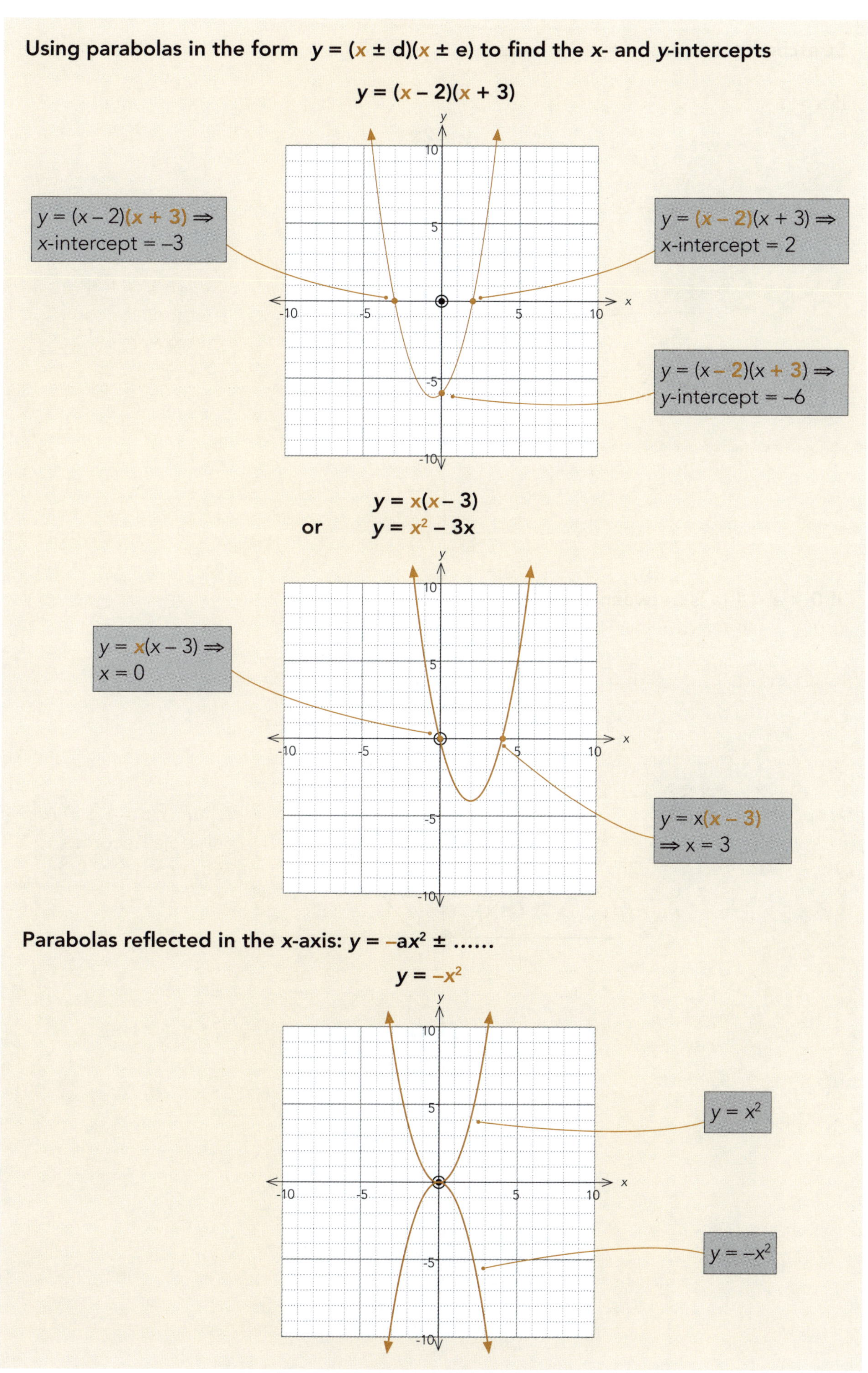
Using parabolas in the form y = (x ± d)(x ± e) to find the x- and y-intercepts
y = (x – 2)(x + 3)
y = (x – 2)(x + 3) ⇒
x-intercept = –3
y = (x – 2)(x + 3) ⇒
x-intercept = 2
y = (x – 2)(x + 3) ⇒
y-intercept = –6
y = x(x – 3)
or y = x² – 3x
y = x(x – 3) ⇒
x = 0
y = x(x – 3)
⇒ x = 3
Parabolas reflected in the x-axis: y = –ax² ± ......
y = –x²
y = x²
y = –x²

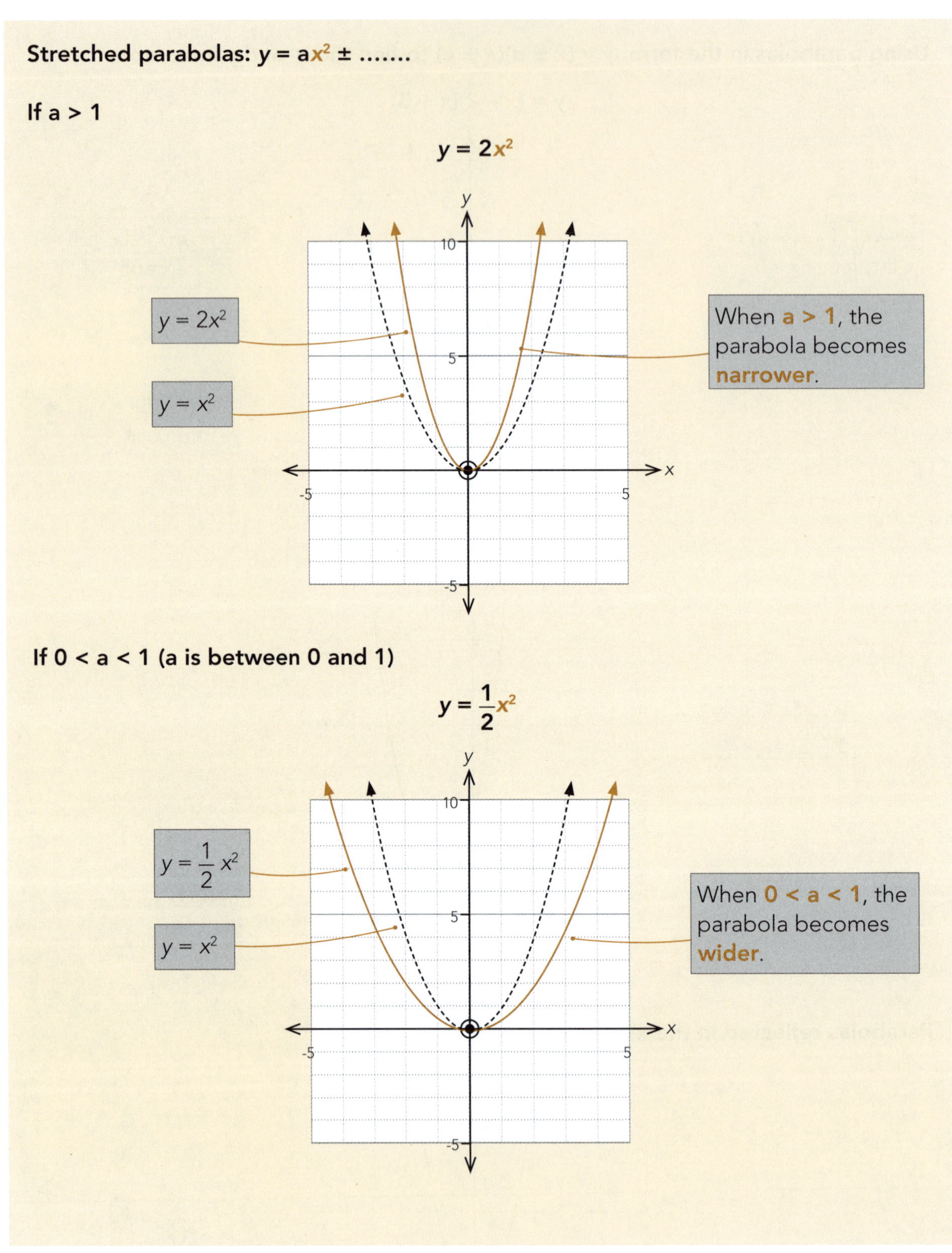

  ISBN: 9780170416009

Parabolas — matching equations with graphs

Use your knowledge from the previous section of the book to match the equations to their respective graphs.

1 **a**

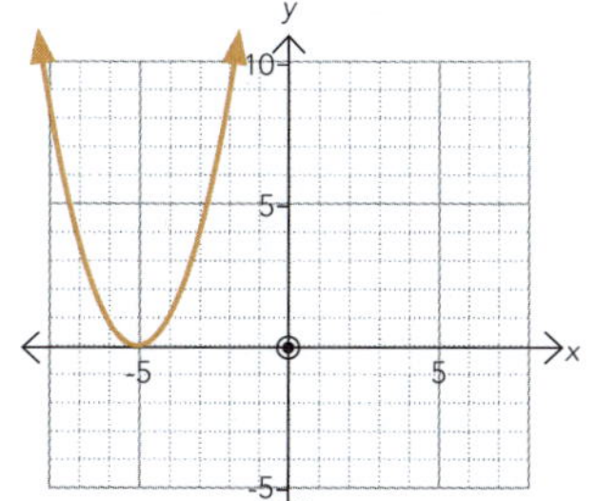

____

b

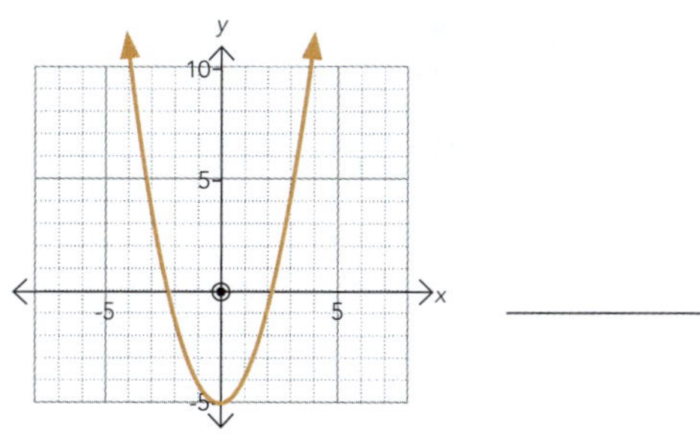

c

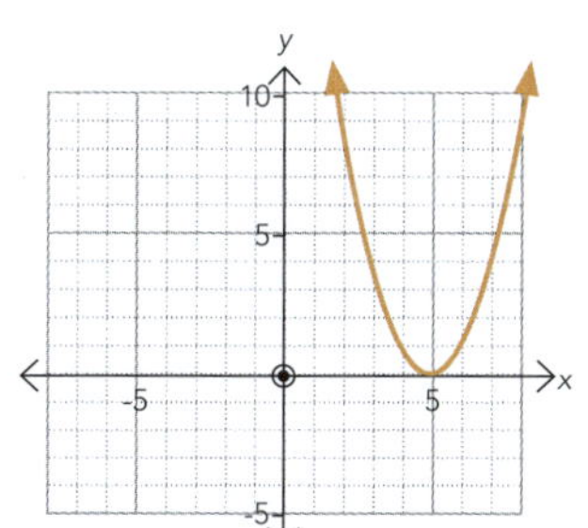

____

d

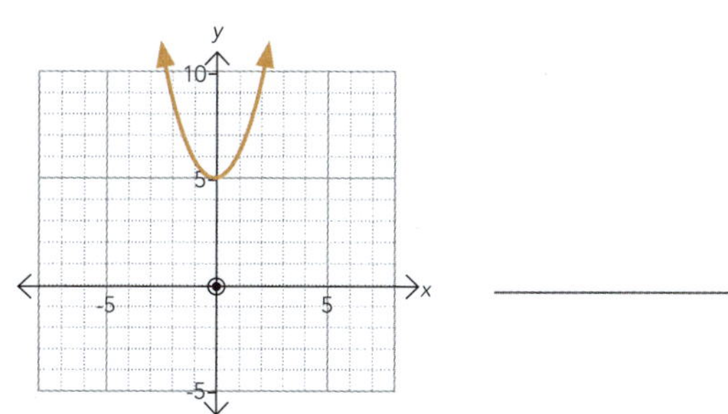

A: $y = x^2 + 5$ **B**: $y = (x - 5)^2$
C: $y = (x + 5)^2$ **D**: $y = x^2 - 5$

2 **a**

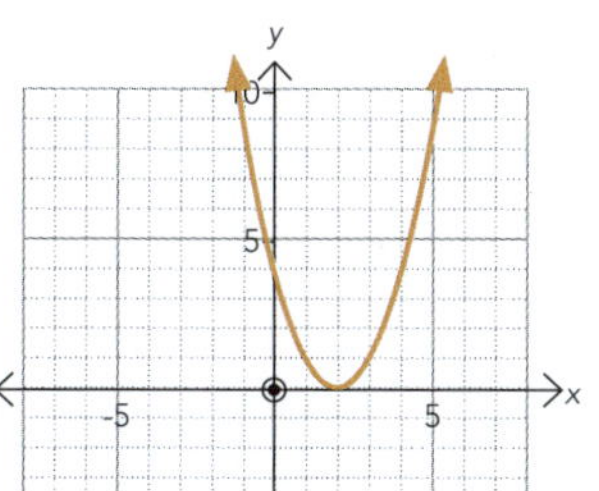

____

b

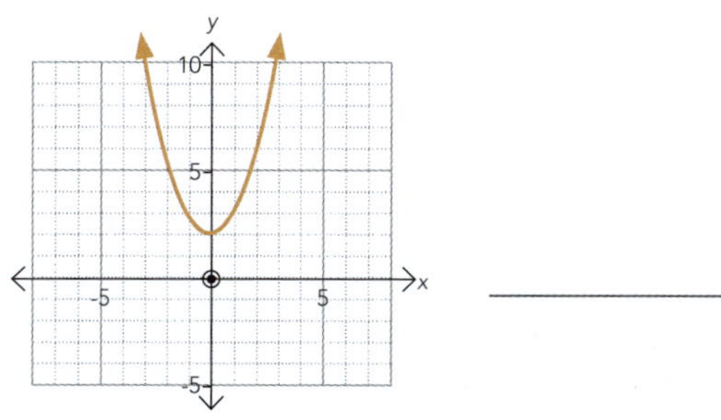

c

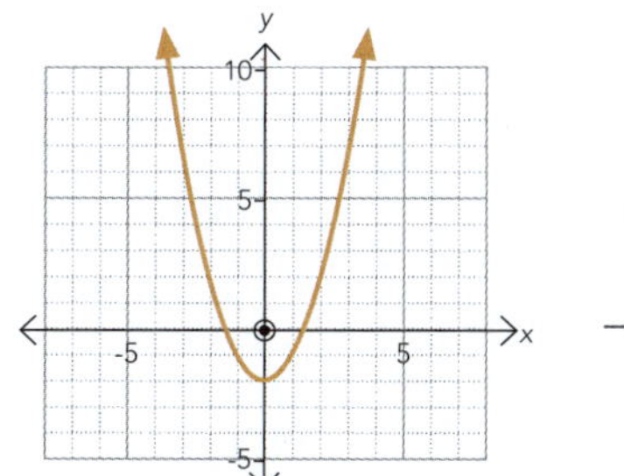

____

d

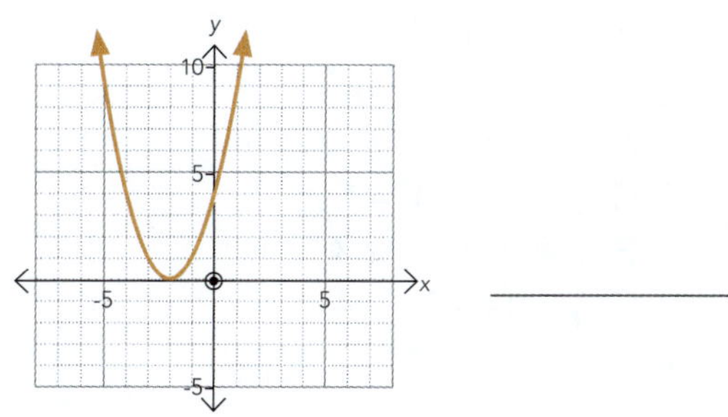

A: $y = x^2 - 2$ **B**: $y = x^2 + 2$
C: $y = (x + 2)^2$ **D**: $y = (x - 2)^2$

ISBN: 9780170416009

3 **a**

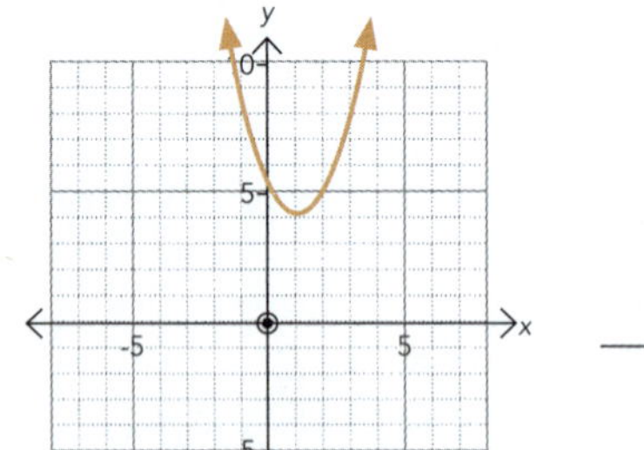

____

b

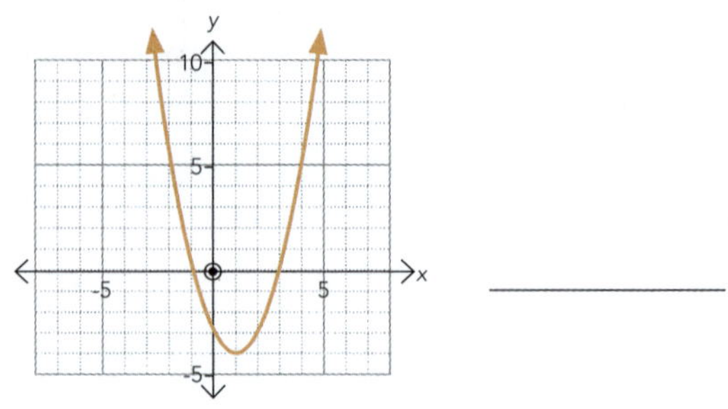

____

c

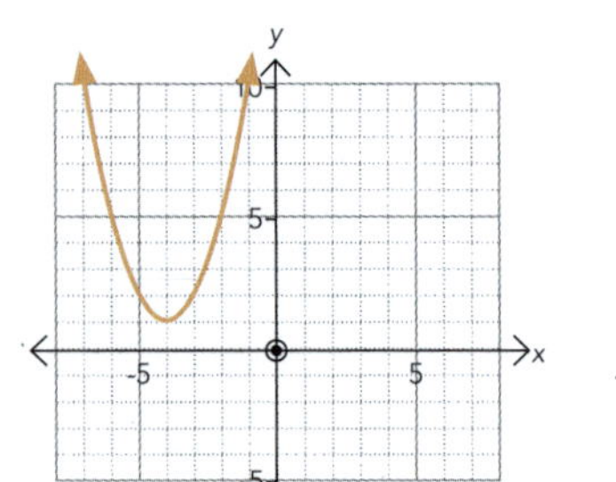

____

d

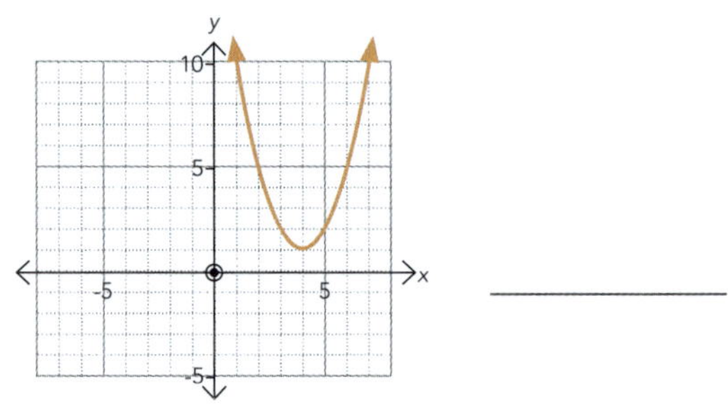

____

e

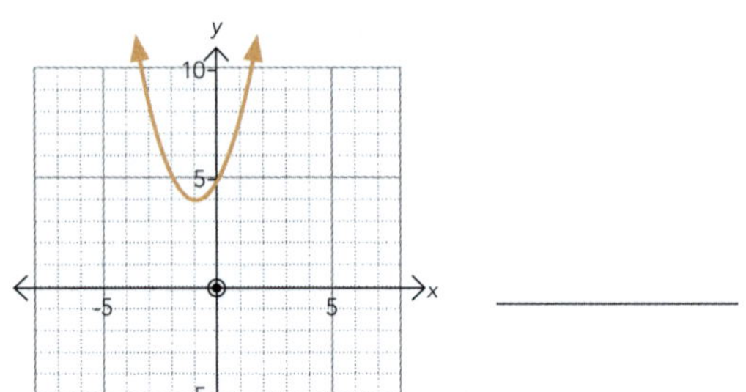

____

f

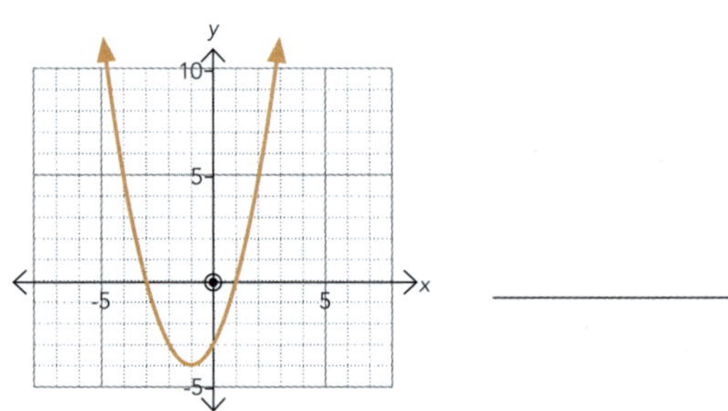

____

g

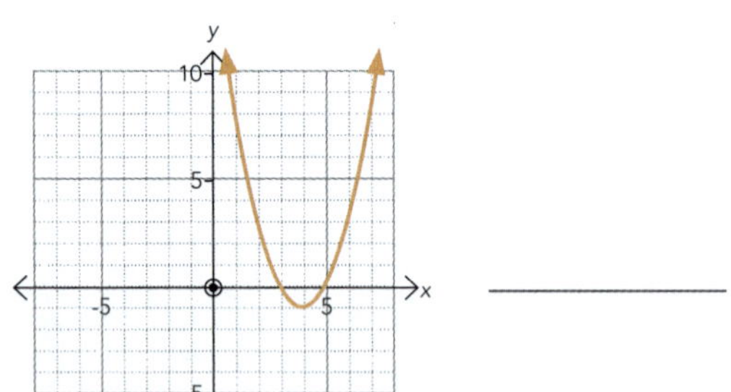

____

h

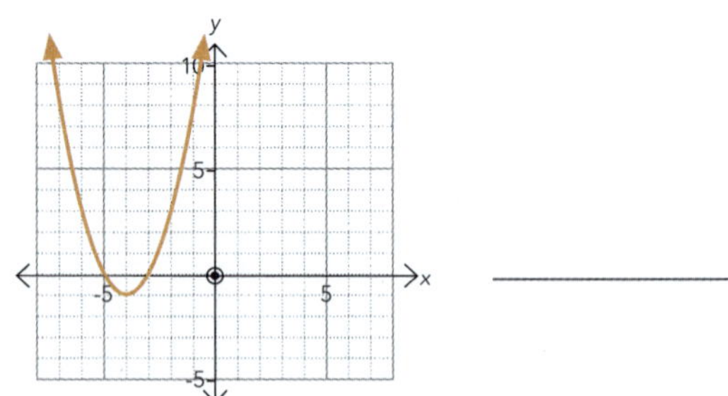

____

A: $y = (x - 1)^2 + 4$

B: $y = (x + 1)^2 - 4$

C: $y = (x - 4)^2 - 1$

D: $y = (x + 4)^2 - 1$

E: $y = (x + 1)^2 + 4$

F: $y = (x + 4)^2 + 1$

G: $y = (x - 1)^2 - 4$

H: $y = (x - 4)^2 + 1$

ISBN: 9780170416009

4 **a**

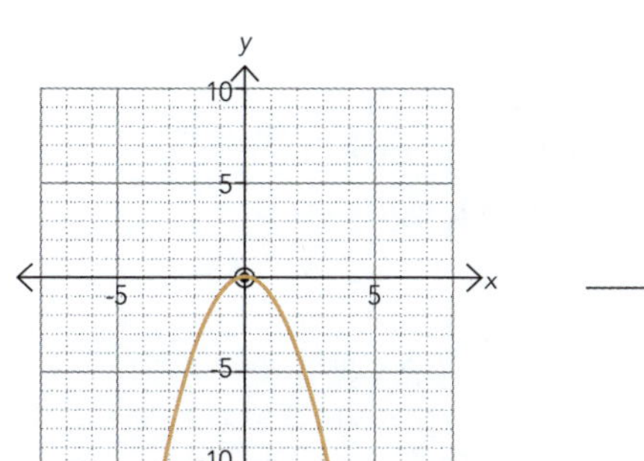

____

b

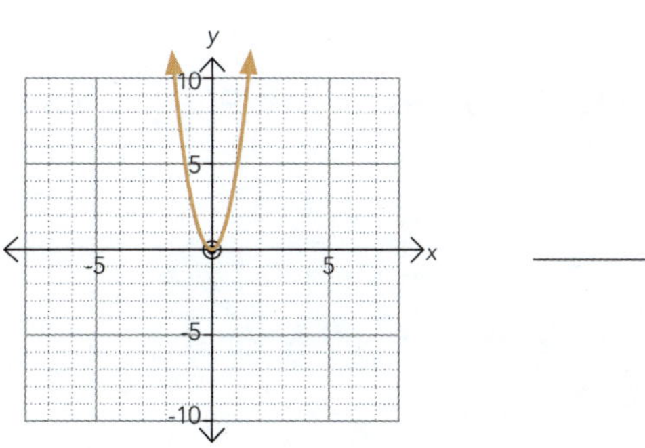

____

c

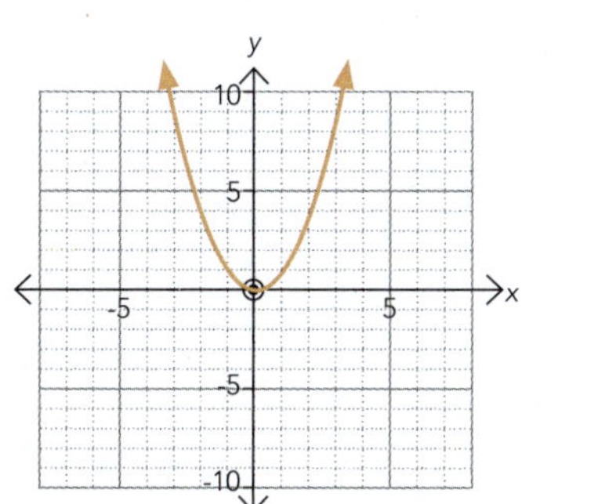

____

d

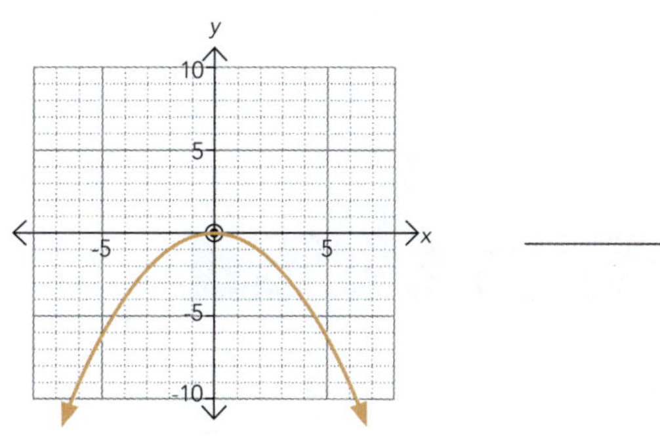

____

e

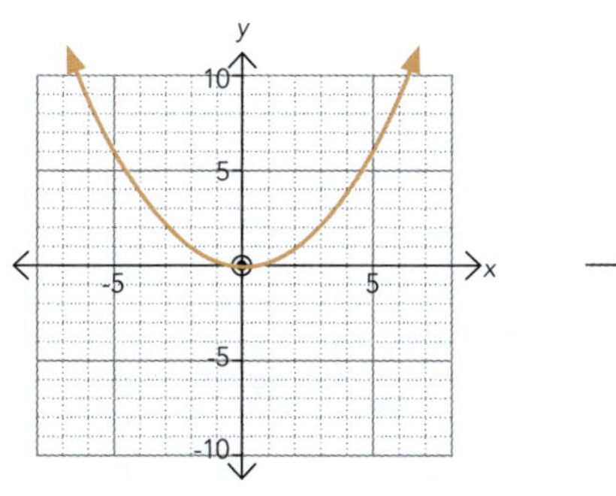

____

f

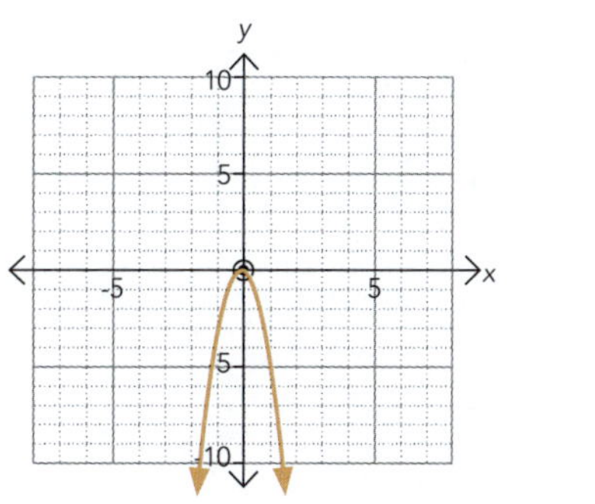

____

A: $y = -4x^2$

B: $y = \frac{1}{4}x^2$

C: $y = x^2$

D: $y = 4x^2$

E: $y = -\frac{1}{4}x^2$

F: $y = -x^2$

ISBN: 9780170416009

Circles

Recognising equations for circles

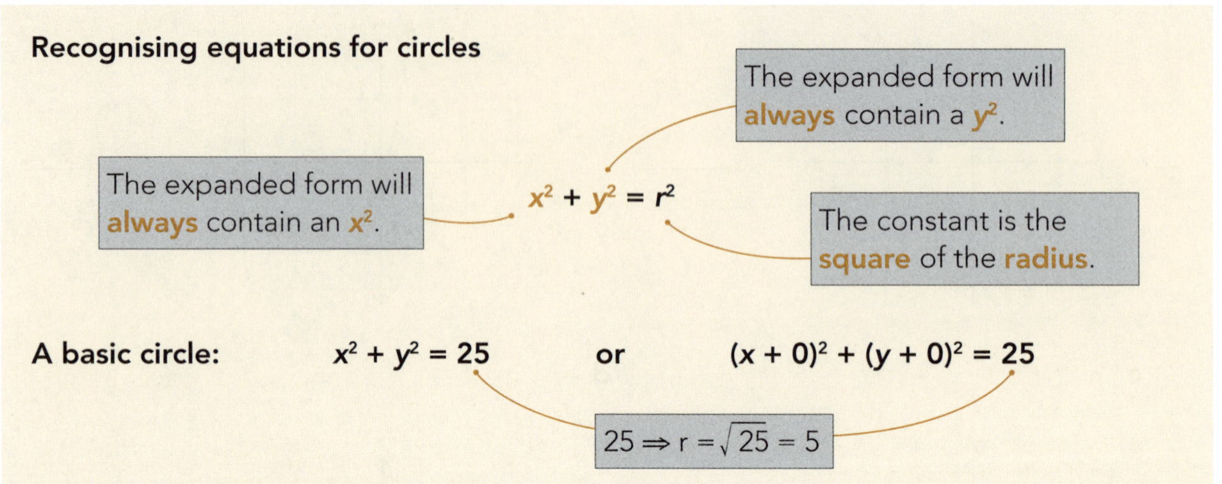

A basic circle: $x^2 + y^2 = 25$ or $(x + 0)^2 + (y + 0)^2 = 25$

$25 \Rightarrow r = \sqrt{25} = 5$

x	$y = \sqrt{25 - x^2}$
0	± 5
3	± 4
4	± 3
5	0
-4	± 3
-3	± 4
-5	0

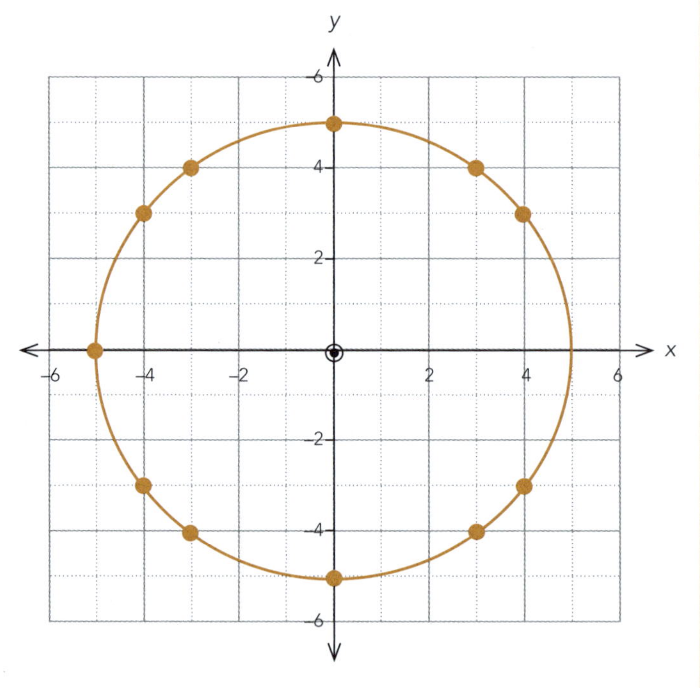

Note: With most circles, you cannot plot as may integral points as for this one.

 ISBN: 9780170416009

Using transformations of circles to find the centre and radius

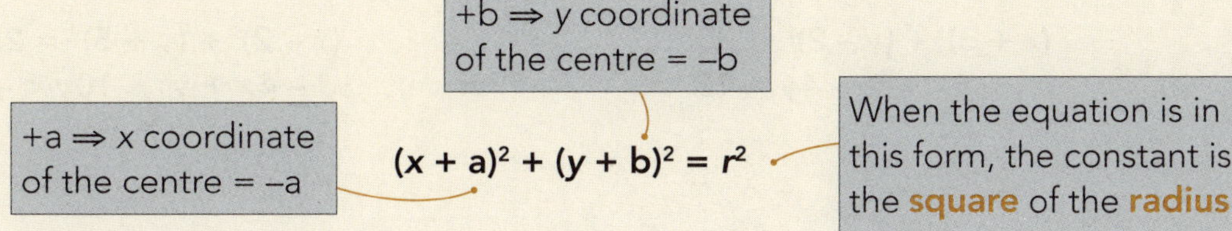

Vertical translation

Notice that the graph moves in the **opposite** direction to the sign.

Notice that expanding the brackets and moving all the constants to the right, means the value on the right of the equals sign is **no longer r^2**.

$$x^2 + (y - 4)^2 = 25$$
or $$(x + 0)^2 + (y - 4)^2 = 25$$
or $$x^2 + y^2 - 8y = 9$$

$$x^2 + (y + 3)^2 = 25$$
or $$(x + 0)^2 + (y + 3)^2 = 25$$
or $$x^2 + y^2 + 6y = 16$$

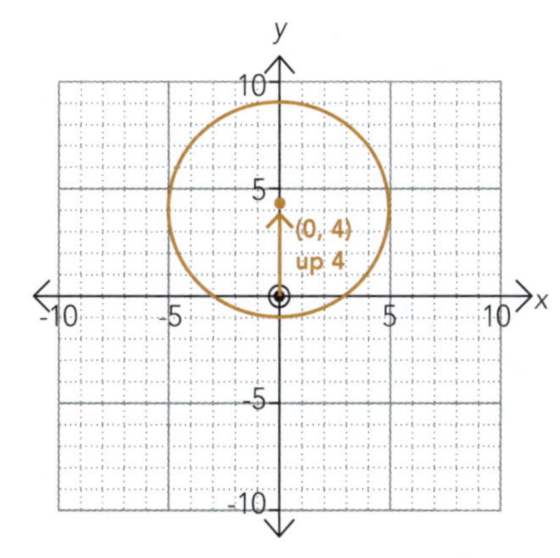

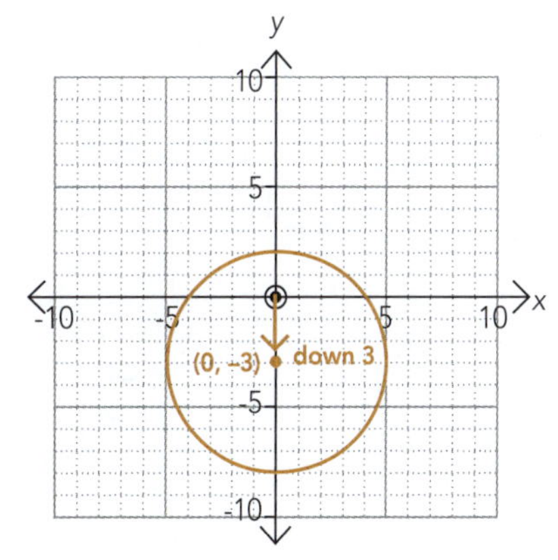

Horizontal translation

Notice that the graph moves in the **opposite** direction to the sign.

$$(x - 4)^2 + y^2 = 25$$
or $$(x - 4)^2 + (y + 0)^2 = 25$$
or $$x^2 - 8x + y^2 = 9$$

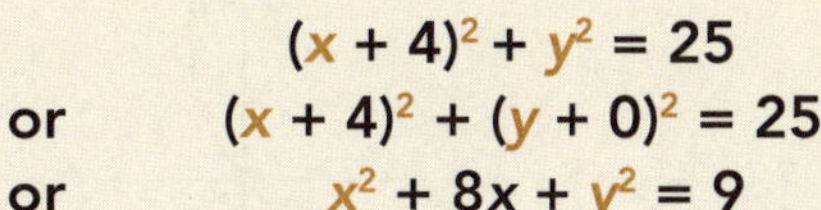

$$(x + 4)^2 + y^2 = 25$$
or $$(x + 4)^2 + (y + 0)^2 = 25$$
or $$x^2 + 8x + y^2 = 9$$

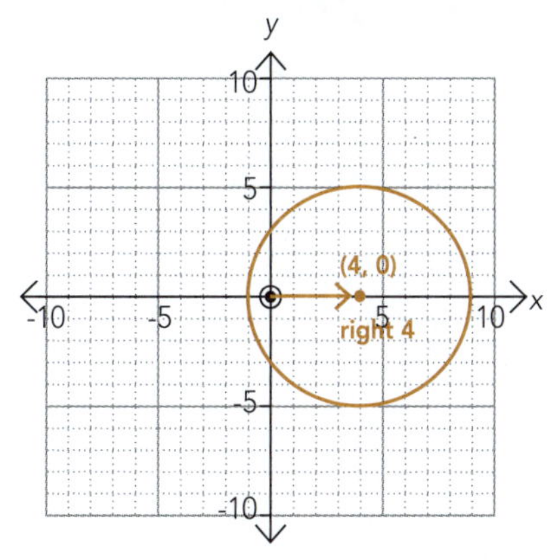

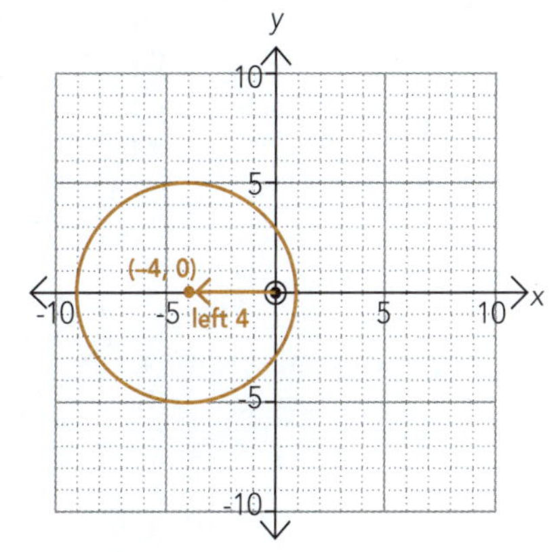

ISBN: 9780170416009

Combinations

$$(x + 3)^2 + (y - 2)^2 = 25$$
or
$$x^2 + 6x + y^2 - 4y = 12$$

$$(x - 2)^2 + (y + 5)^2 = 25$$
or
$$x^2 - 4x + y^2 + 10y = -4$$

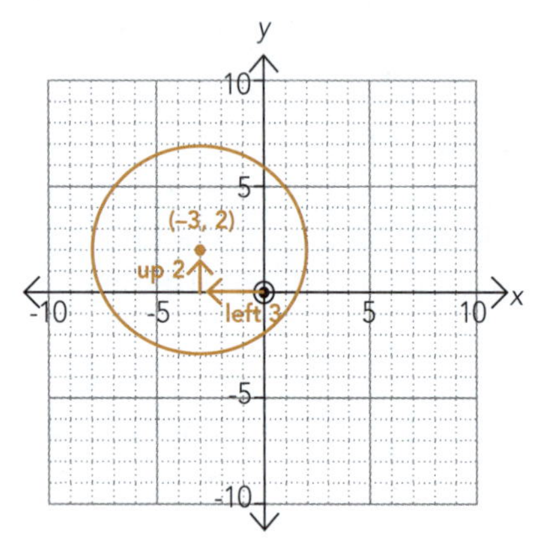

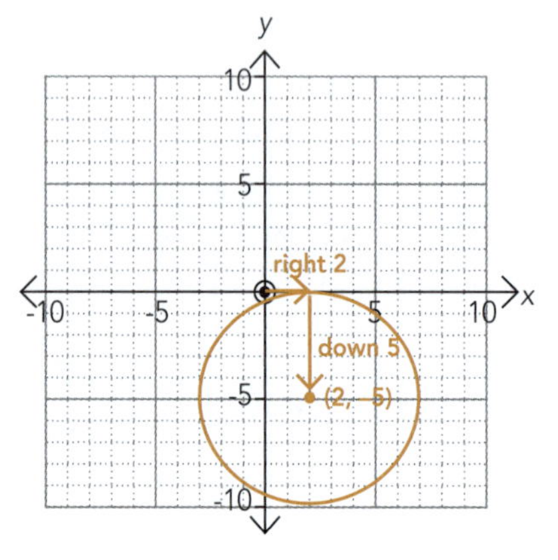

Using equations in the form $x^2 \pm ax + y^2 \pm by = 0$ to find the x- and y-intercepts

$$x^2 + 8x + y^2 - 7y = 0$$
or
$$x(x + 8) + y(y - 7) = 0$$
or
$$(x + 0)(x + 8) + (y + 0)(y - 7) = 0$$

$(x + 0)(x + 8) + (y + 0)(y - 7) = 0$
$\Rightarrow$ y-intercept = +7

$(x + 0)(x + 8) + (y + 0)(y - 7) = 0$
$\Rightarrow$ x and y-intercepts = 0

$(x + 0)(x + 8) + (y + 0)(y - 7) = 0$
$\Rightarrow$ x-intercept = –8

ISBN: 9780170416009

Circles — matching equations with graphs

Use your knowledge from the previous section of the book to match the equations to their respective graphs.

1 **a**

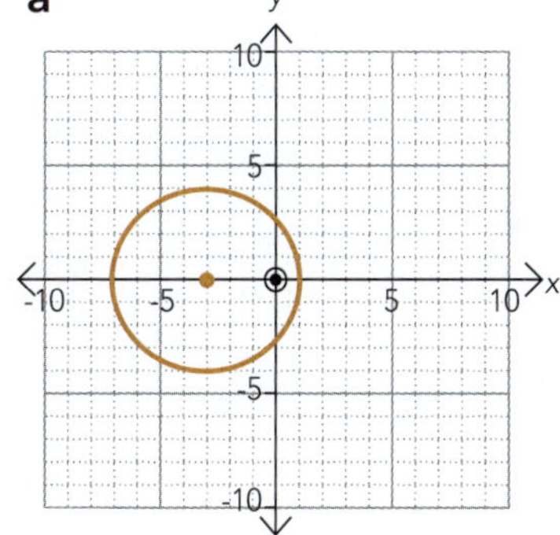

______

b

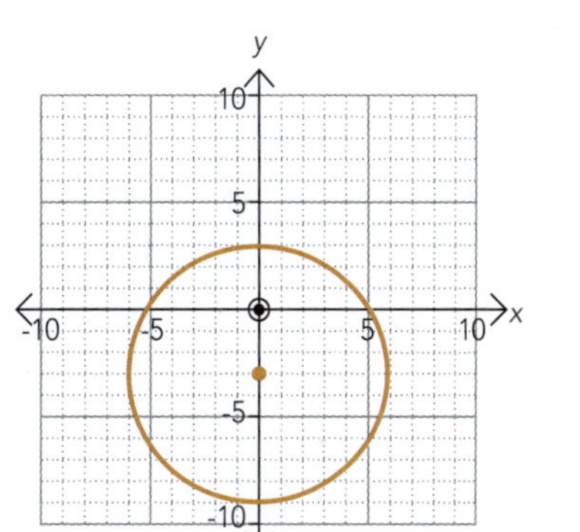

______

c

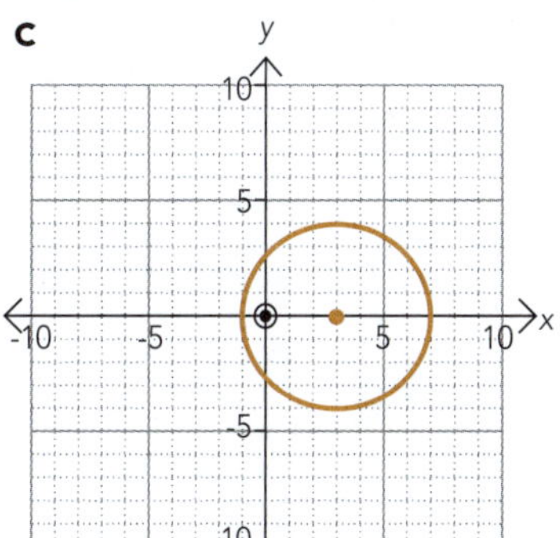

______

d

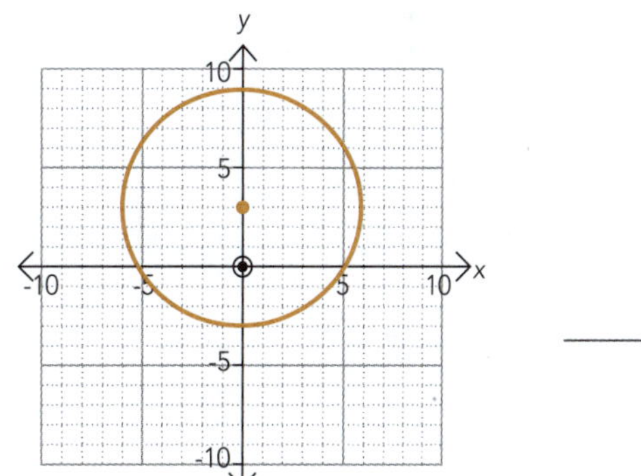

______

e

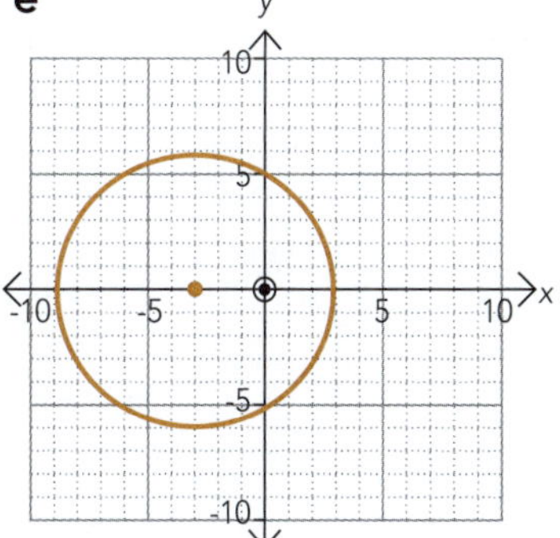

______

f

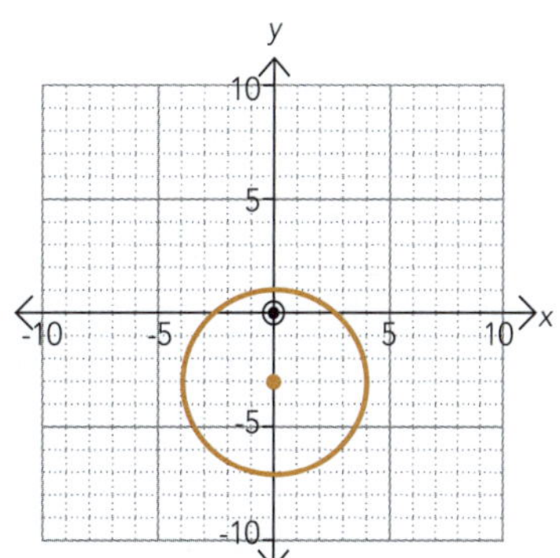

______

g

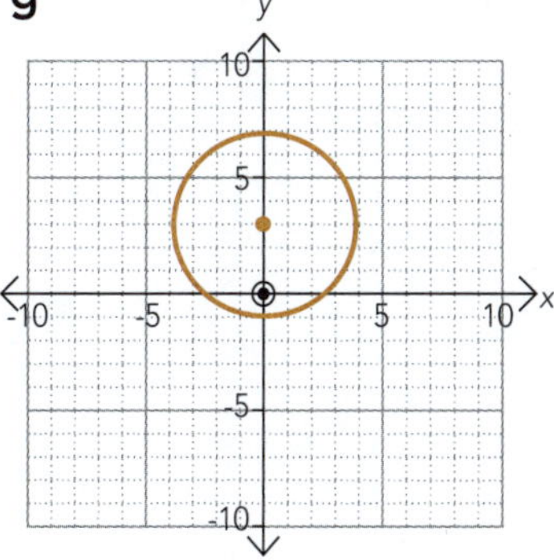

______

h

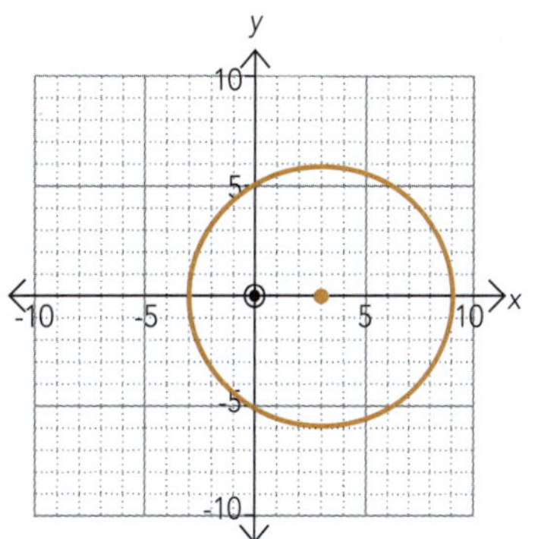

______

A: $(x + 3)^2 + y^2 = 16$

B: $x^2 + (y - 3)^2 = 16$

C: $x^2 + (y + 3)^2 = 16$

D: $(x + 3)^2 + y^2 = 36$

E: $(x - 3)^2 + y^2 = 36$

F: $(x - 3)^2 + y^2 = 16$

G: $x^2 + (y - 3)^2 = 36$

H: $x^2 + (y + 3)^2 = 36$

ISBN: 9780170416009

2 **a**

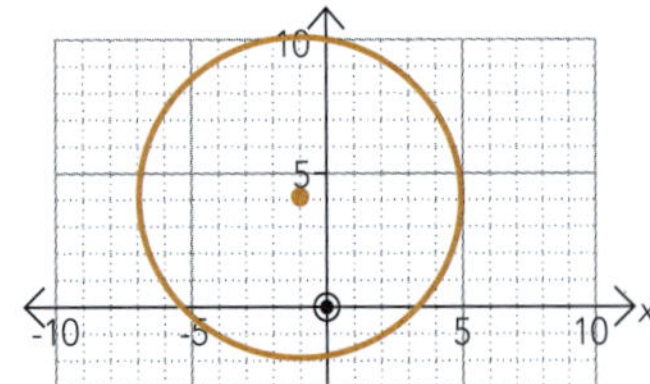

______

b

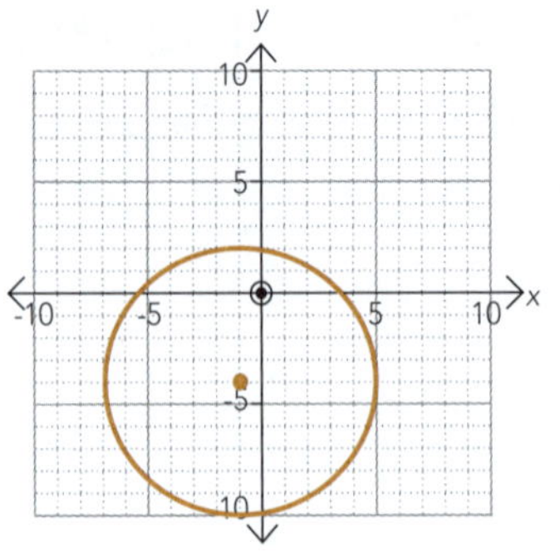

______

c

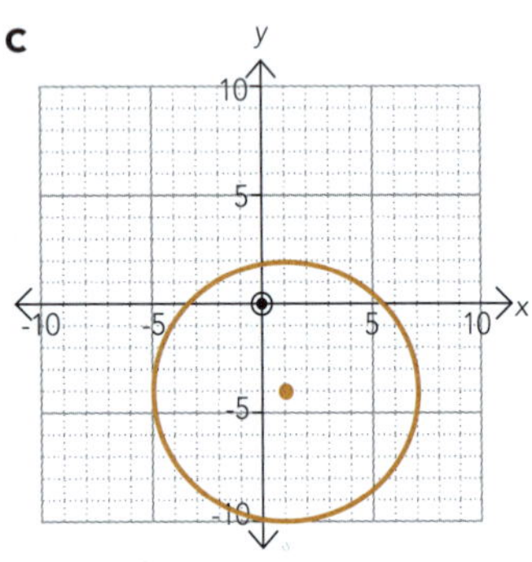

______

d

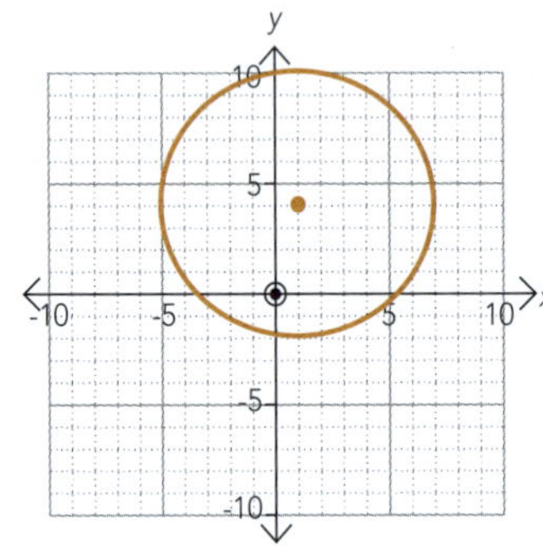

______

A: $(x-1)^2+(y+4)^2=36$

B: $(x-1)^2+(y-4)^2=36$

C: $(x+1)^2+(y+4)^2=36$

D: $(x+1)^2+(y-4)^2=36$

3 **a**

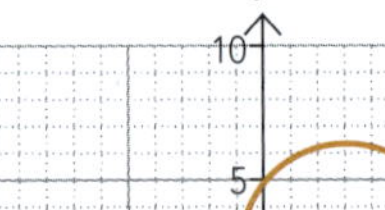

______

b

Hint: use intercepts for these questions.

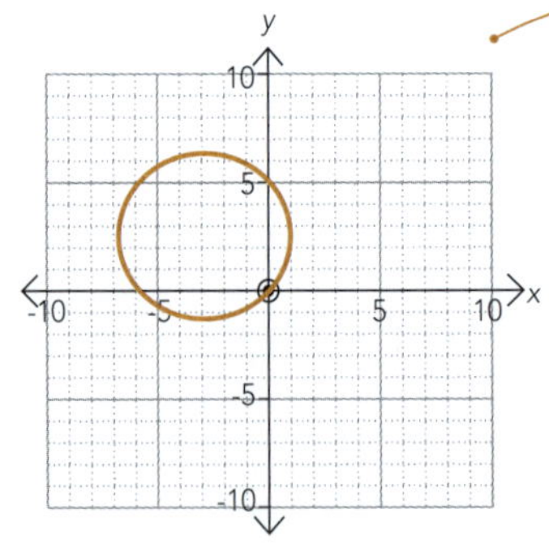

______

c

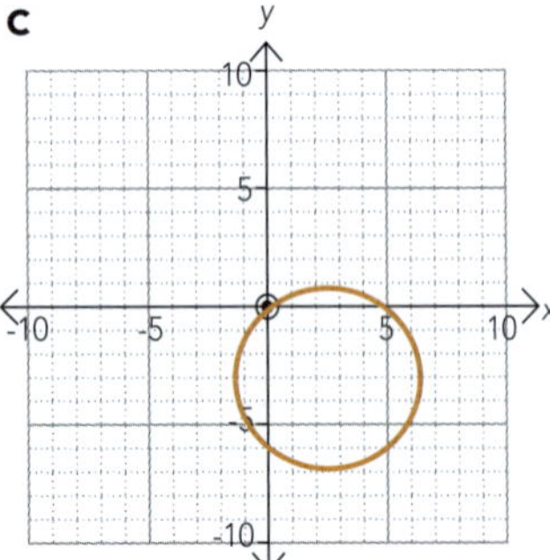

______

d

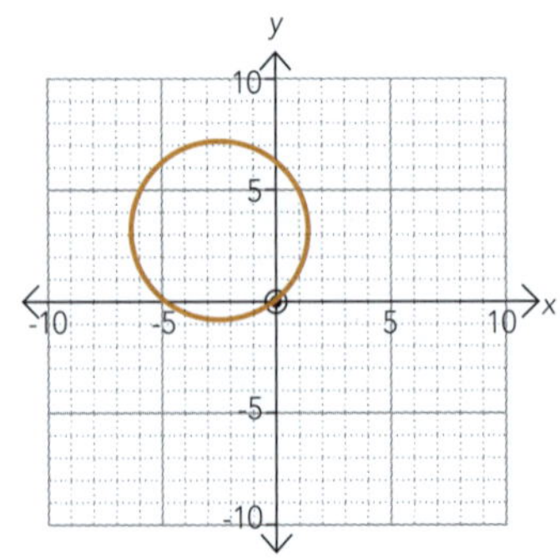

______

A: $x^2+5x+y^2-6y=0$

B: $x^2+6x+y^2-5y=0$

C: $x^2-6x+y^2-5y=0$

D: $x^2-5x+y^2+6y=0$

ISBN: 9780170416009

Hyperbolas

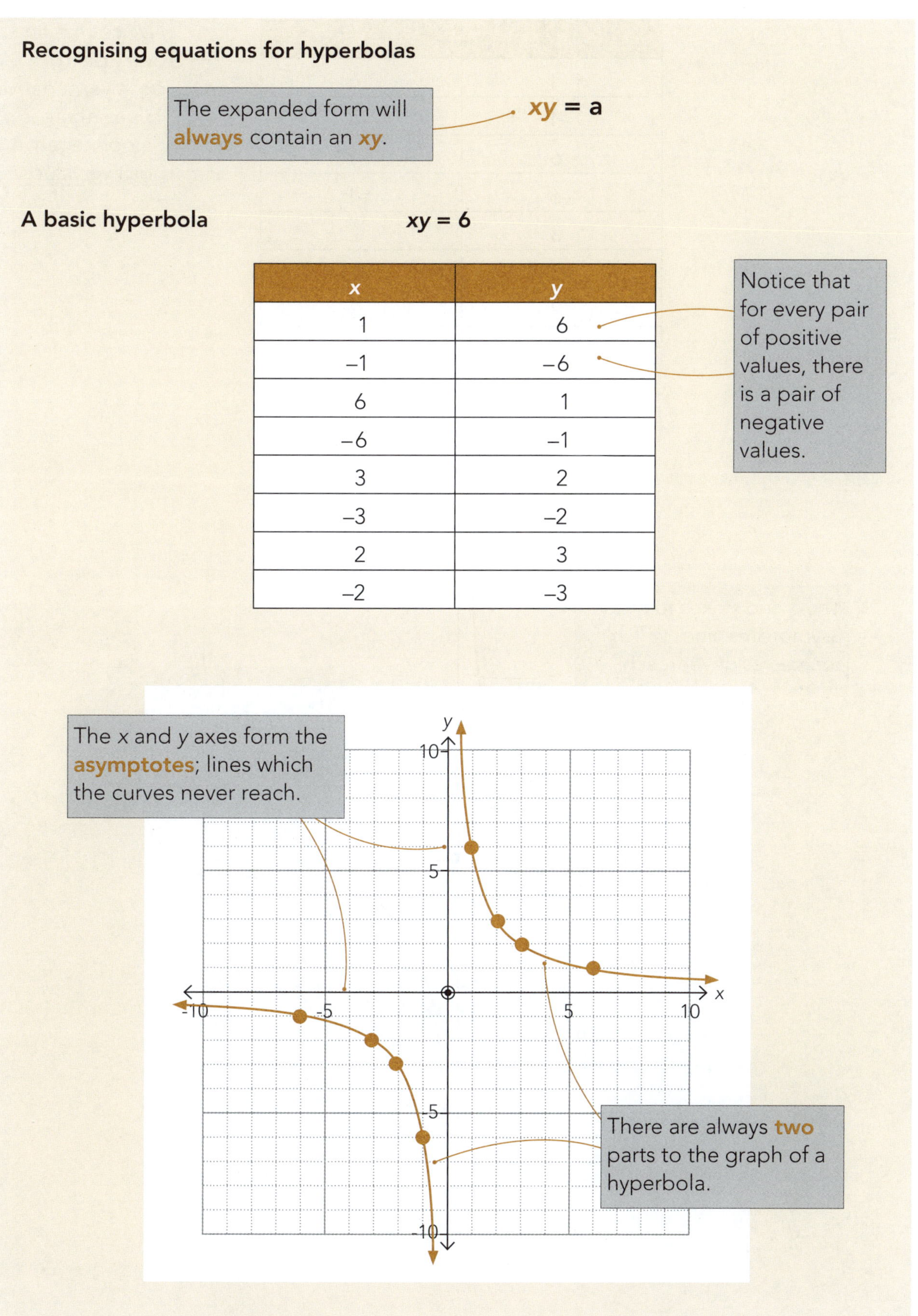

Recognising equations for hyperbolas

The expanded form will **always** contain an **xy**.

$$xy = a$$

A basic hyperbola

$$xy = 6$$

x	y
1	6
–1	–6
6	1
–6	–1
3	2
–3	–2
2	3
–2	–3

Notice that for every pair of positive values, there is a pair of negative values.

ISBN: 9780170416009

A hyperbola where the constant is negative: $xy = -6$

x	y
1	6
–1	–6
6	1
–6	–1
3	2
–3	–2
2	3
–2	–3

Notice that for every pair of positive/negative values, there is a pair of negative/positive values.

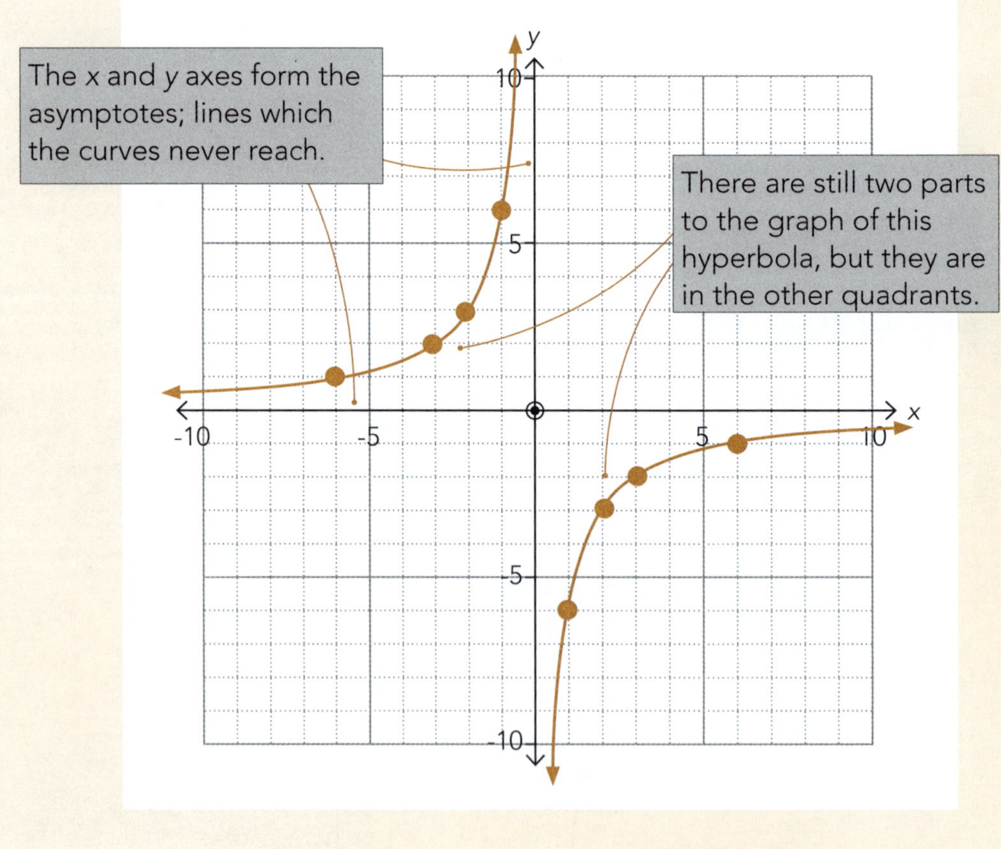

ISBN: 9780170416009

Using transformations of hyperbolas to find where the asymptotes cross

Vertical translation

Notice that the graph moves in the **opposite** direction to the sign.

The size of the constant (6) determines how 'tight' the curve is, not its position.

$x(y + 5) = 6$
or $xy + 5x = 6$

$x(y - 3) = 6$
or $xy - 3x = 6$

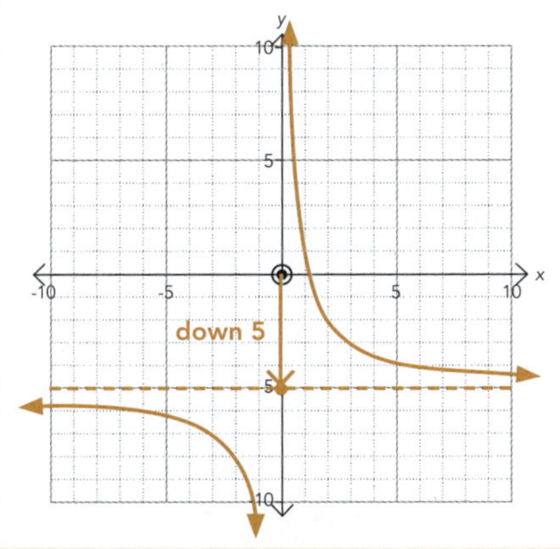

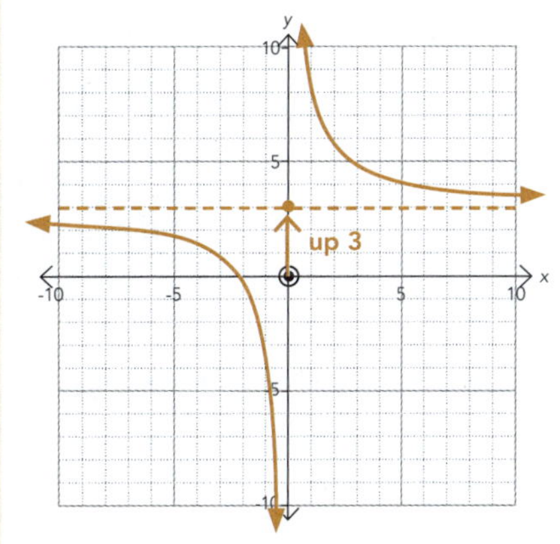

Horizontal translation

Notice that the graph moves in the **opposite** direction to the sign.

$(x + 3)y = 6$
or $xy + 3y = 6$

$(x - 5)y = 6$
or $xy - 5y = 6$

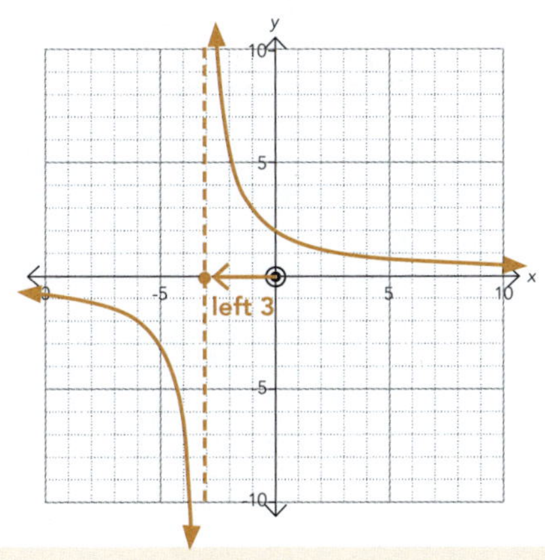

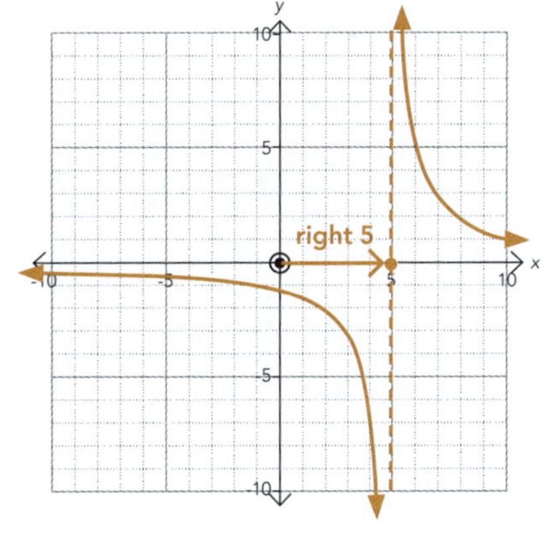

Combinations

$(x - 2)(y + 5) = 6$

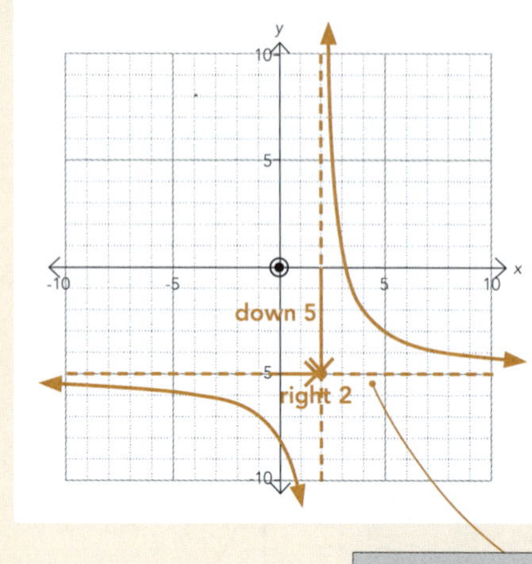

$(x + 4)(y - 3) = 6$

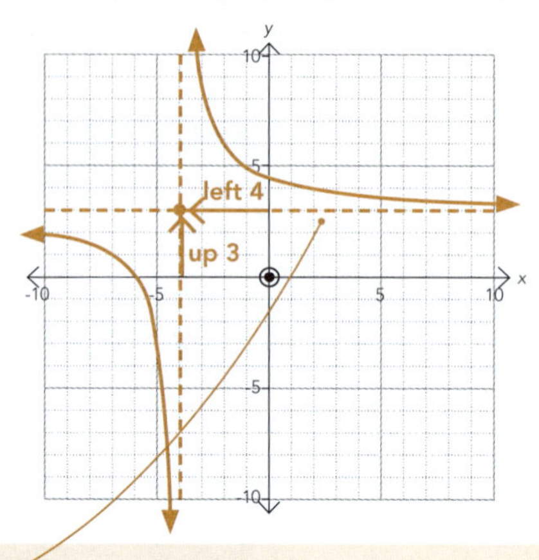

Drawing the asymptotes makes finding the equation easier.

Changing the size of the constant

Notice that the coordinates of each point are factors of the constant.

e.g. $3 \times 5 = 15$

$6 \times 6 = 36$

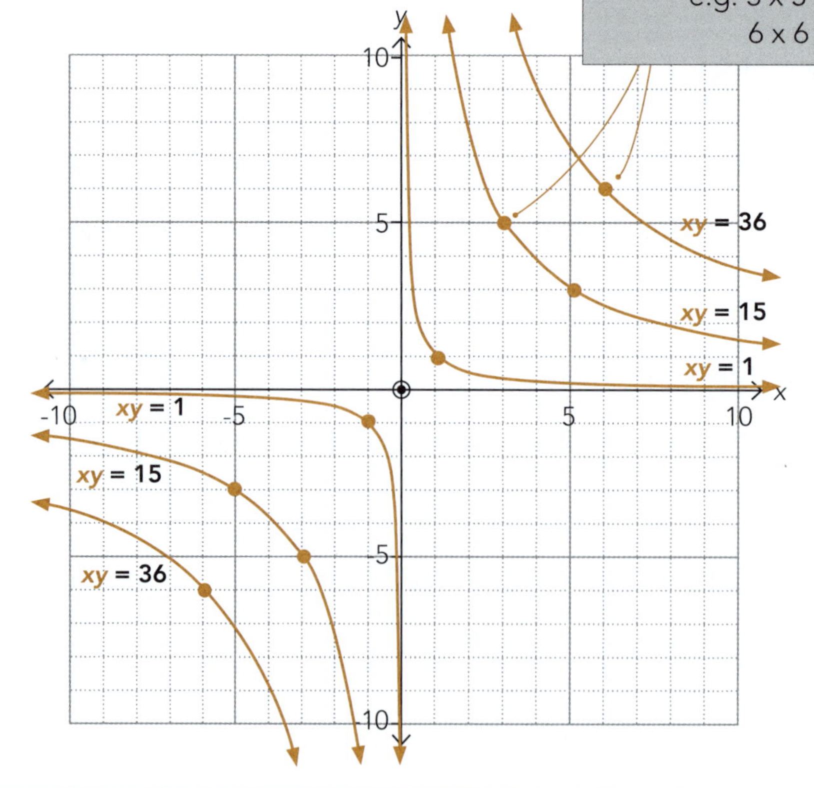

  ISBN: 9780170416009

Hyperbolas — matching equations with graphs

Use your knowledge from the previous section of the book to match the equations to their respective graphs.

1 **a**

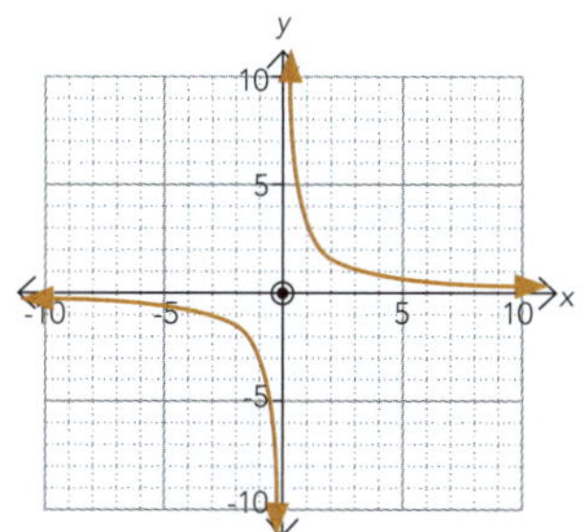

______

b

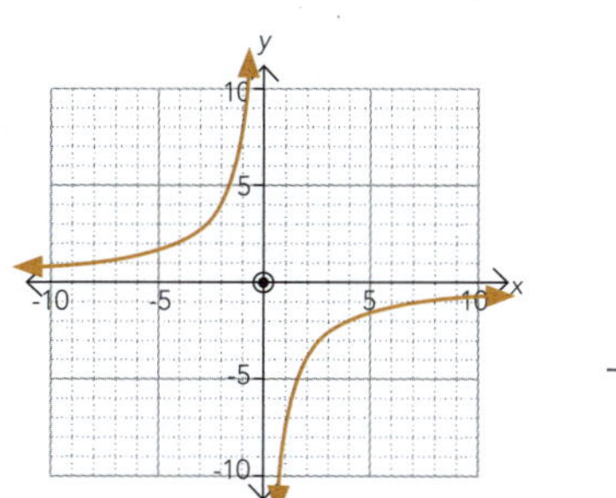

______

c

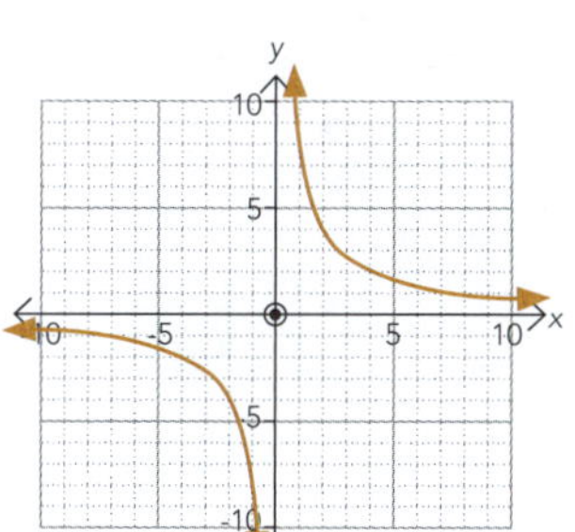

______

d

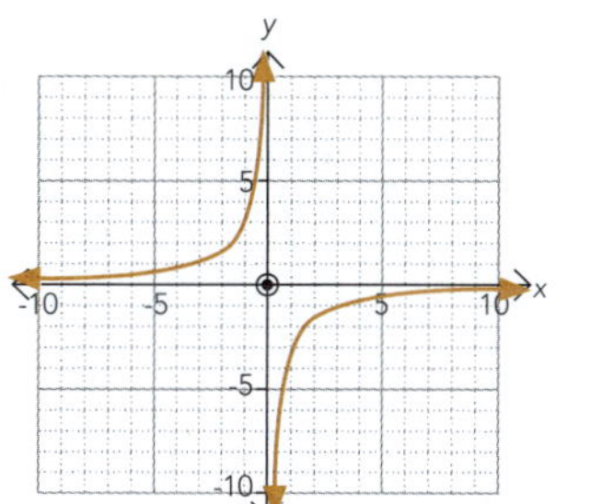

______

A: $xy = -8$
C: $xy = 8$
B: $xy = -3$
D: $xy = 3$

2 **a**

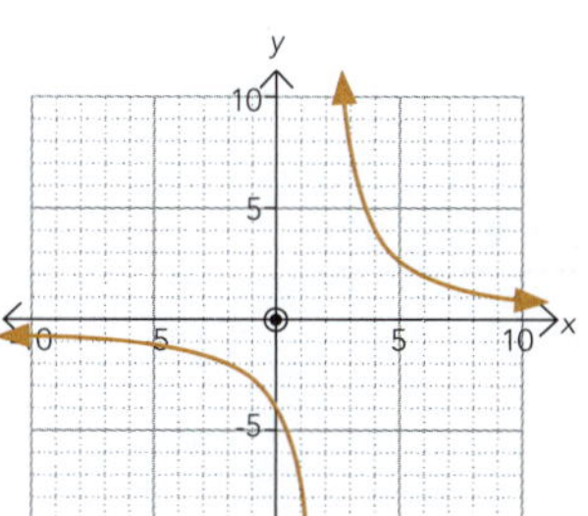

______

b

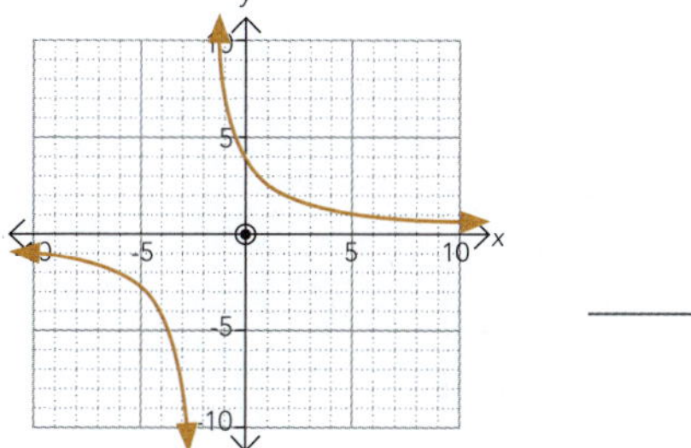

______

c

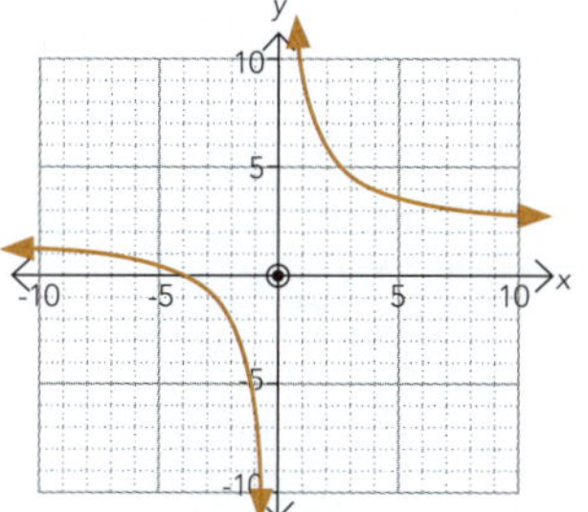

______

d

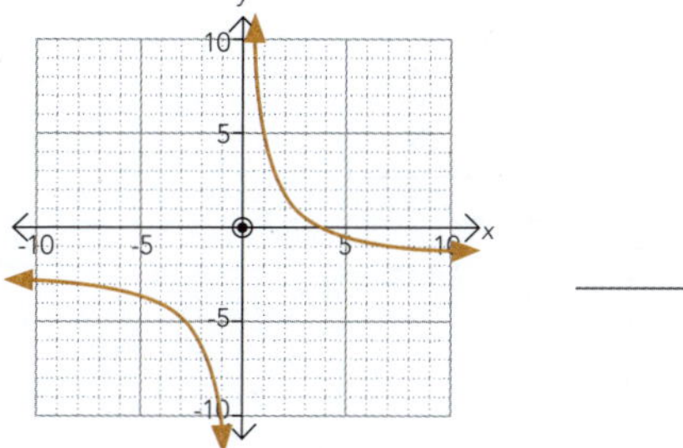

______

A: $x(y + 2) = 8$
C: $(x + 2)y = 8$
B: $x(y - 2) = 8$
D: $(x - 2)y = 8$

ISBN: 9780170416009

3 **a**

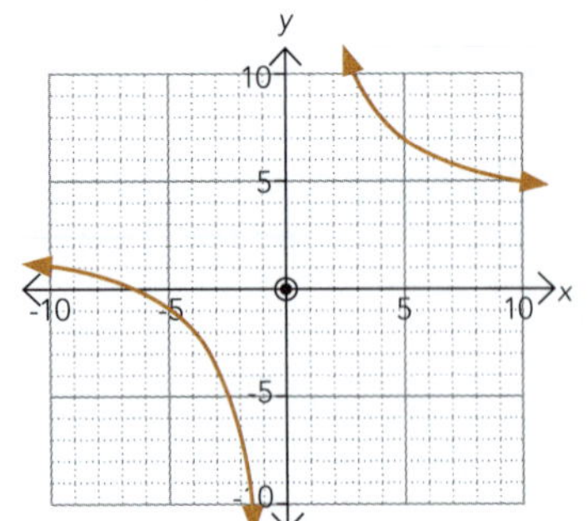

______

b

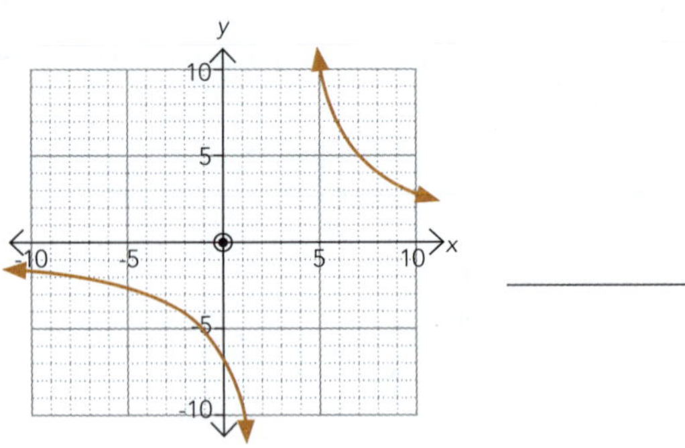

______

c

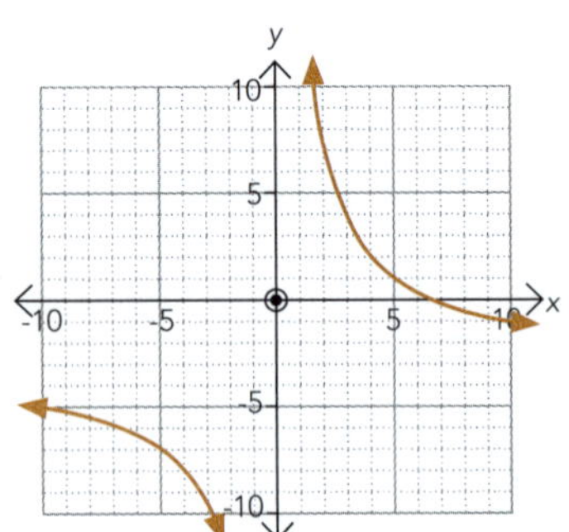

______

d

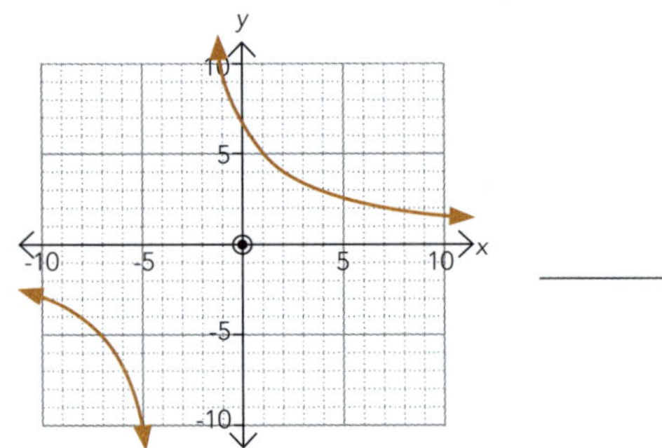

______

A: $(x - 3)y = 20$
C: $x(y - 3) = 20$

B: $x(y + 3) = 20$
D: $(x + 3)y = 20$

4 **a**

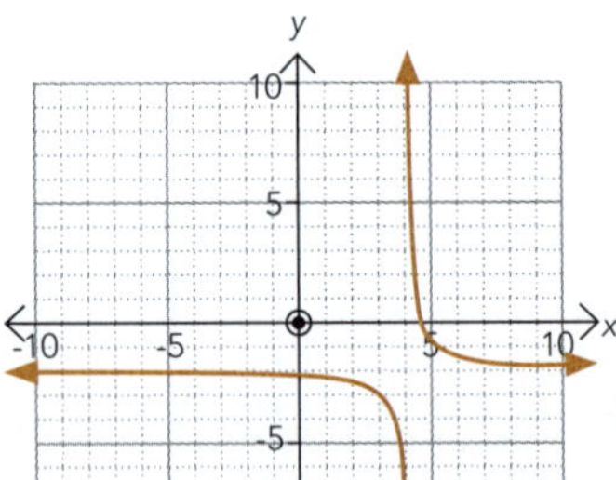

______

b

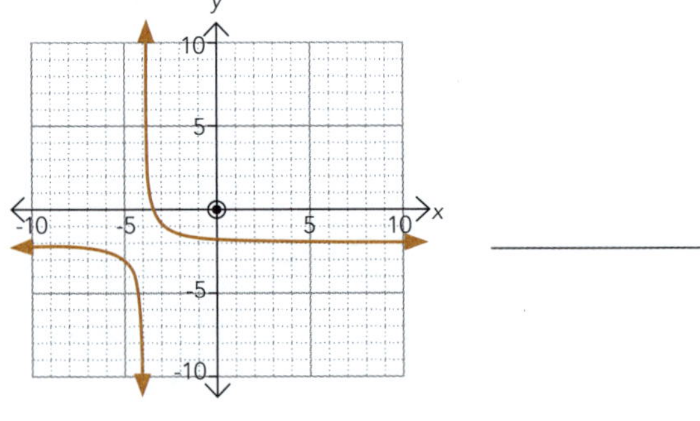

______

c

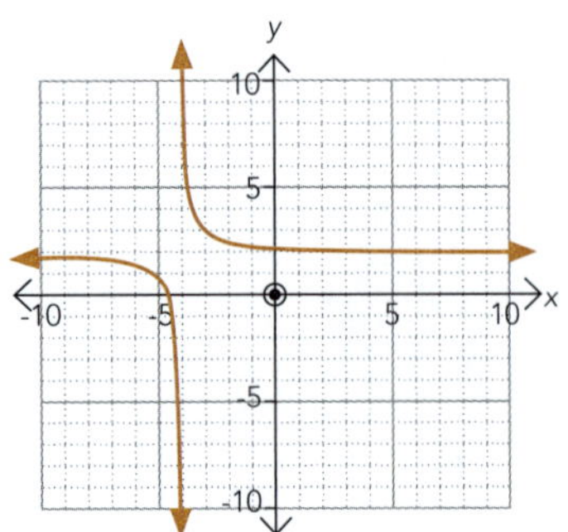

______

d

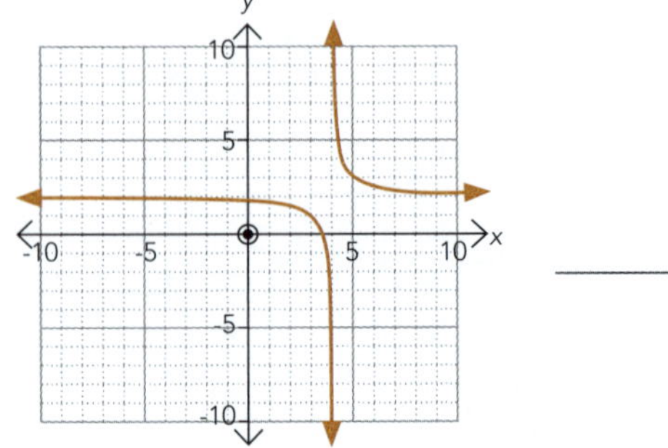

______

A: $(x + 4)(y - 2) = 1$
C: $(x - 4)(y - 2) = 1$

B: $(x - 4)(y + 2) = 1$
D: $(x + 4)(y + 2) = 1$

ISBN: 9780170416009

Mixing it up

Use your knowledge from the previous section of the book to match the equations to their respective graphs.

1 **a**

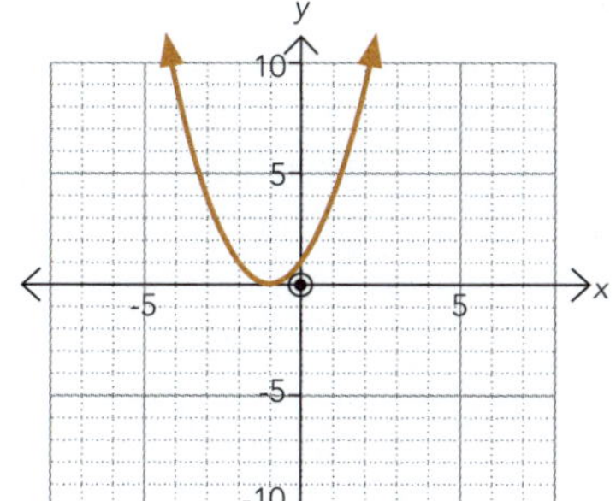

______

b

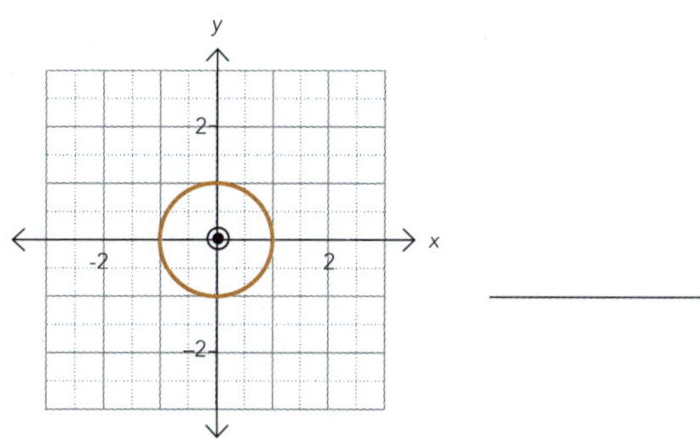

______

c

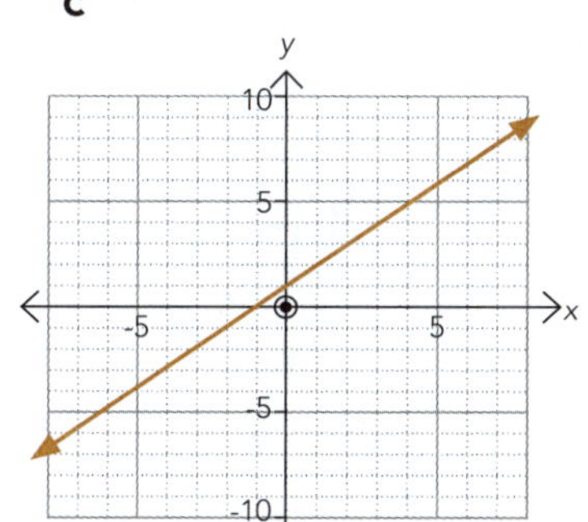

______

d

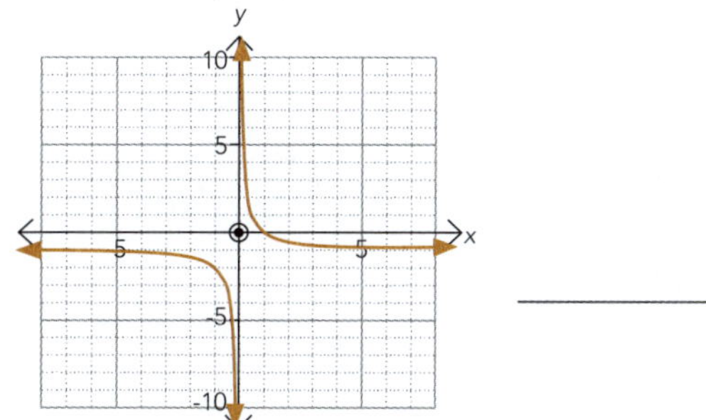

______

e

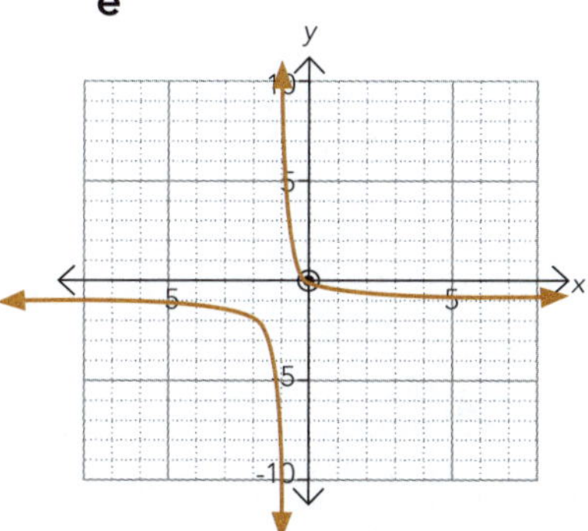

______

f

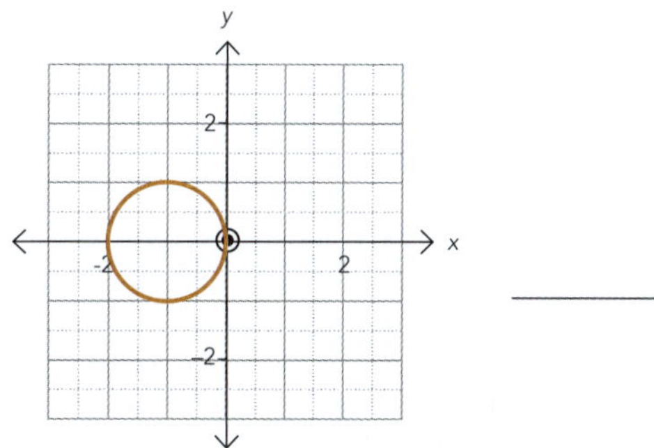

______

g

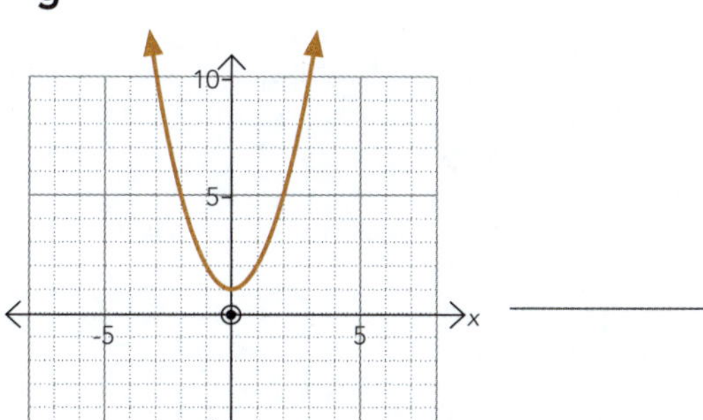

______

h

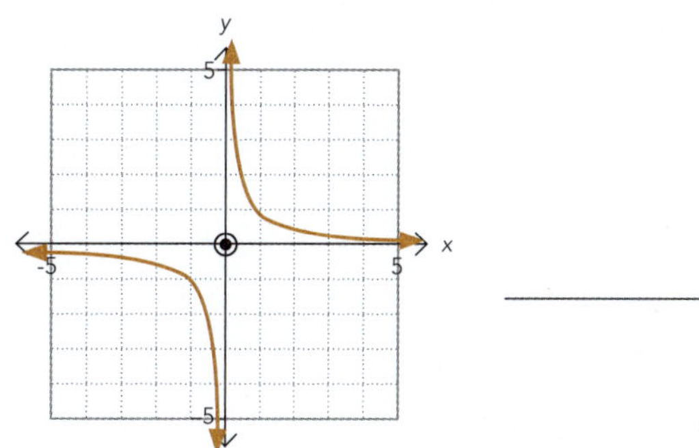

______

A: $y = x + 1$

B: $xy = 1$

C: $x^2 + y^2 = 1$

D: $y = x^2 + 1$

E: $y = (x + 1)^2$

F: $(x + 1)^2 + y^2 = 1$

G: $x(y + 1) = 1$

H: $(x + 1)(y + 1) = 1$

ISBN: 9780170416009

2 **a**

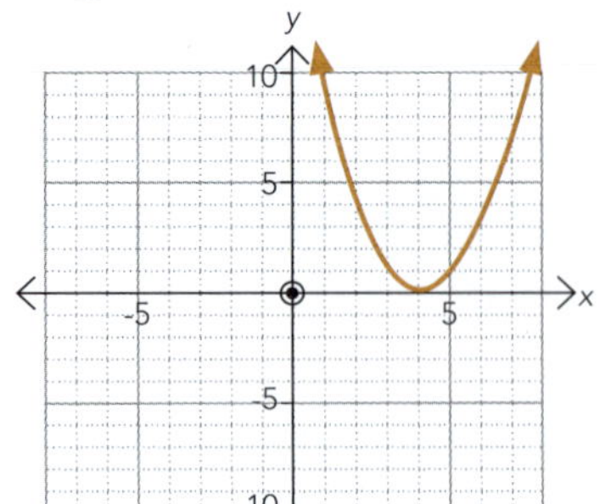

______

b

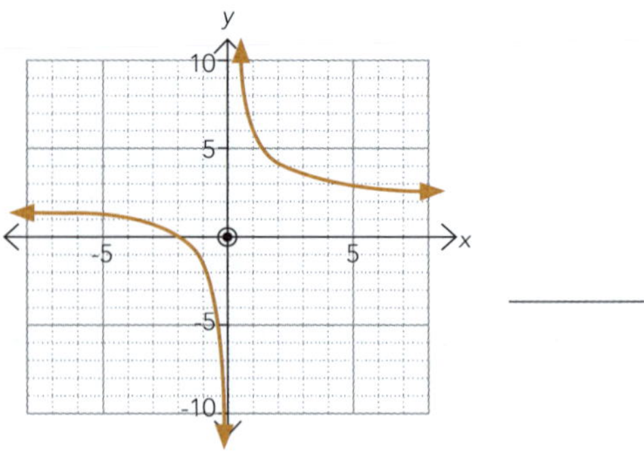

______

c

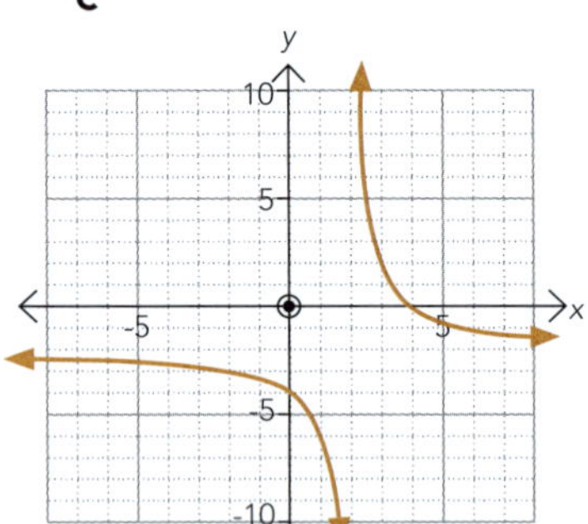

______

d

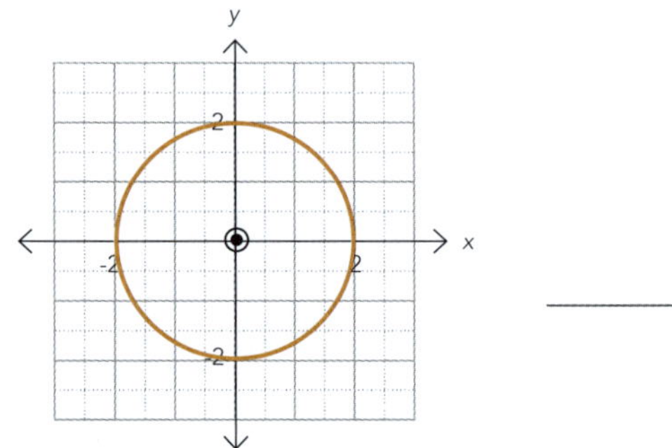

______

e

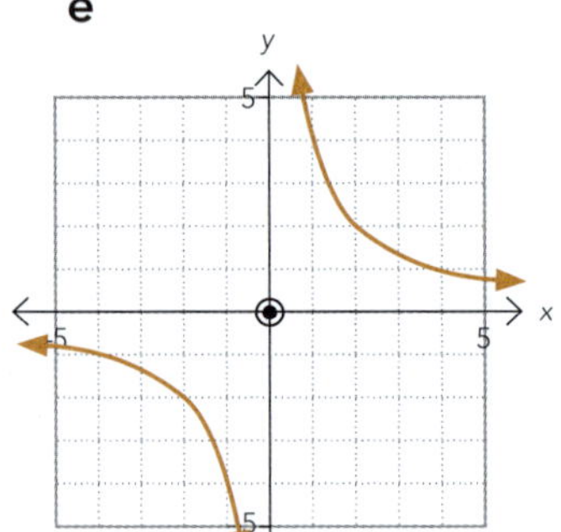

______

f

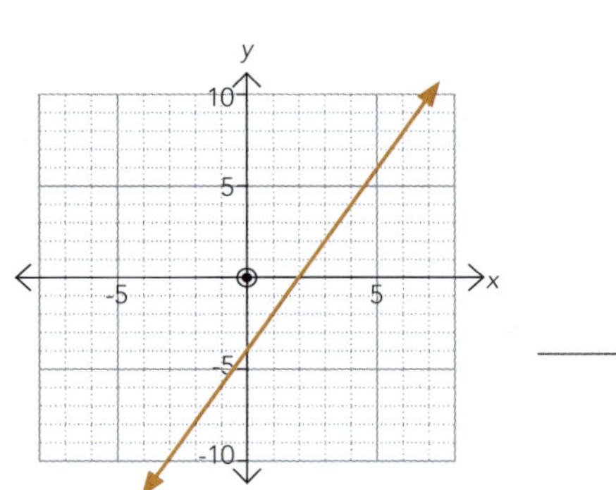

______

g

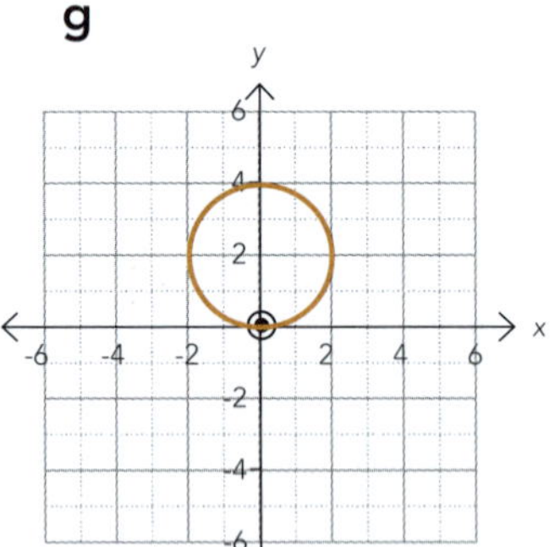

______

h

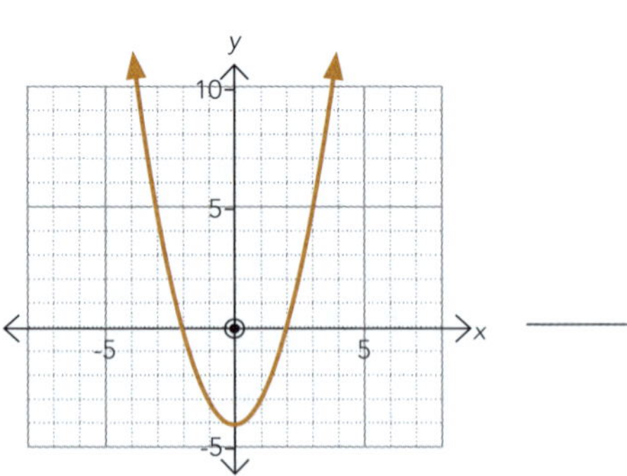

______

A: $y = 2x - 4$

B: $xy = 4$

C: $x^2 + y^2 = 4$

D: $y = x^2 - 4$

E: $y = (x - 4)^2$

F: $x^2 + (y - 2)^2 = 4$

G: $x(y - 2) = 4$

H: $(x - 2)(y + 2) = 4$

ISBN: 9780170416009

Quadratic expressions

Expanding

Remember **FOIL**:

Firsts
Outers
Inners
Lasts

F O I L

Example: $(x + 3)(2x - 5) = 2x^2 - 5x + 6x - 15$
$= 2x^2 + x - 15$

Combine like terms.

Examples:

1 $(2x - 4)(3x - 5) = 6x^2 - 10x - 12x + 20$
$= 6x^2 - 22x + 20$

2 $(2x + 3)(2x - 3) = 4x^2 - 6x + 6x - 9$
$= 4x^2 + 0x - 9$
$= 4x^2 - 9$

3 $(x + 7)^2 = (x + 7)(x + 7)$
$= x^2 + 7x + 7x + 49$
$= x^2 + 14x + 49$

4 $(4x - 2)^2 = (4x - 2)(4x - 2)$
$= 16x^2 - 8x - 8x + 4$
$= 16x^2 - 16x + 4$

Expand and simplify these.

1 $(x + 3)(x + 2)$

2 $(x + 5)(x - 2)$

3 $(4 + x)(x + 7)$

4 $(x + 9)^2$

ISBN: 9780170416009

5 $(x + 1)(3x - 2)$

6 $(4x - 3)(2x + 5)$

7 $(3x - 4)^2$

8 $(5 - x)^2$

9 $(3 + 2x)(1 - x)$

10 $-(x + 3)(4x - 5)$

11 $(6x - 3)(3x + 5)$

12 $(11 - 3x)(4 + 7x)$

13 $(x + 3)(x - 3)$

14 $(4x - 7)(4x + 7)$

15 $(5 - 2x)(5 + 2x)$

16 $(10x + 5)^2$

ISBN: 9780170416009

Factorising quadratics

1 Where the coefficient of x^2 is 1

1 List all the factors of the constant: $x^2 + 3x - 40$

1, 40
2, 20
4, 10
5, 8

2 Select the pair that could add or subtract to give the coefficient of x: $x^2 + 3x - 40$

$-5 + 8 = +3$

3 The factors are $(x - 5)(x + 8)$

4 **Check** your answer by expanding the brackets using **FOIL** — you should get the original expression: $(x - 5)(x + 8) = x^2 + 3x - 40$

Examples:

1 $x^2 - 11x + 30 = (x - 5)(x - 6)$

1, 30
2, 15
3, 10
−5, −6

2 $x^2 - 7x - 18 = (x + 2)(x - 9)$

1, 18
+2, −9
3, 6

3 $x^2 - 25 = x^2 + 0x - 25 = (x + 5)(x - 5)$

1, 25
+5, −5

Insert a 'fake' x term.

Factorise the following.

1 $x^2 + 7x + 10$

2 $x^2 + 15x + 36$

3 $x^2 + 10x + 9$

4 $x^2 + 4x - 12$

ISBN: 9780170416009

5 $x^2 + 14x + 48$

6 $x^2 - 10x + 21$

7 $x^2 - 5x - 24$

8 $24 + 10x + x^2$

9 $x^2 - 49$

10 $1 - x^2$

11 $x^2 - 12x + 36$

12 $25 - x^2$

13 $9 - 4y^2$

14 $-x^2 + 100$

15 $-x^2 - 5x - 6$

16 $-x^2 - 5x + 6$

17 $-x^2 + 6x - 8$

18 $36 - 16x^2$

ISBN: 9780170416009

2 Where the coefficient of x^2 is not 1, but there is a common factor

Steps:

1 Take out the **common factor** first: $2x^2 - 4x - 6 = \mathbf{2}(x^2 - 2x - 3)$

2 Factorise the part inside the bracket: $= 2(x - 3)(x + 1)$

Examples:

1 $6x^2 + 18x - 60 = 6(x^2 + 3x - 10)$
$= 6(x + 5)(x - 2)$

2 $-3x^2 + 18x - 24 = -3(x^2 - 6x + 8)$
$= -3(x - 4)(x - 2)$

3 $-7x^2 + 28 = -7(x^2 - 4)$
$= -7(x + 2)(x - 2)$

4 $27x^2 - 75 = 3(9x^2 - 25)$
$= 3(3x + 5)(3x - 5)$

Factorise the following.

1 $3x^2 + 9x - 30$

2 $2x^2 - 98$

3 $-4x^2 + 4$

4 $200 - 8x^2$

5 $-5x^2 - 10x - 5$

6 $-4x^2 - 16x - 12$

7 $2x^2 - 2x - 12$

8 $5x^2 - 180$

ISBN: 9780170416009

3 Where the coefficient of x^2 is not 1 and there is no common factor

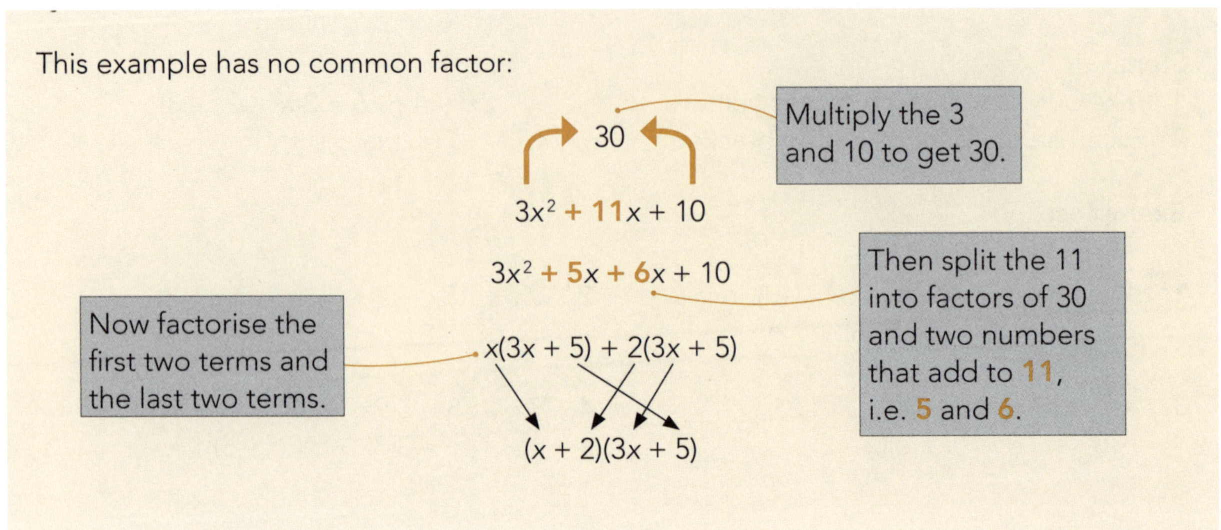

Factorise the following.

1 $3x^2 + 17x + 10$

2 $2x^2 + 11x + 12$

3 $15x^2 + 11x + 2$

4 $3x^2 + 14x - 5$

5 $4x^2 - 27x - 7$

6 $5x^2 - 16x + 3$

ISBN: 9780170416009

7 $4x^2 - 16x - 9$

8 $6x^2 - 13x - 5$

9 $20x^2 - 7x - 6$

10 $21x^2 - 41x + 10$

11 $-2x^2 + x + 6$

12 $-5x^2 + 21x - 4$

13 $-6x^2 - x + 35$

14 $4x^2 - 25$

15 $36x^2 - 49$

16 $4x^2 + 36x + 81$

17 $25 + 9x^2 - 30x$

18 $8 - 35x^2 - 6x$

ISBN: 9780170416009

Solving quadratic equations

1 By factorising

Example:

$2x^2 + 5x = 3$

Step 1: Rearrange so that 0 is on the right: $2x^2 + 5x - 3 = 0$

Step 2: Factorise: $(2x - 1)(x + 3) = 0$

This means one bracket **multiplied** by the other. If **$a \times b$** = 0, then either **$a = 0$** or **$b = 0$**.

Step 3: Solve by considering what happens when each bracket equals 0.

Either $(2x - 1) = 0$ or $(x + 3) = 0$

$2x = 1$ $x = -3$

$x = \frac{1}{2}$

So, if $2x^2 + 5x = 3$, then x is either $\frac{1}{2}$ or -3.

Note: Most quadratic equations that you come across will have **two solutions**. Some have just **one solution**. This can be thought of as **two identical solutions**. Some have **no real solutions**.

Examples:

1 Two solutions:

$$x^2 - 3x - 10 = 0$$
$$(x + 2)(x - 5) = 0$$
$$x = -2 \text{ or } 5$$

$$6x^2 + 5x - 6 = 0$$
$$(2x + 3)(3x - 2) = 0$$
Either $2x + 3 = 0$
$$x = -\frac{3}{2}$$
or $3x - 2 = 0$
$$x = \frac{2}{3}$$

$$x^2 - 16 = 0$$
$$(x + 4)(x - 4) = 0$$
$$x = -4$$
or $x = 4$

2 One solution (or two identical solutions):

$$x^2 + 10x + 25 = 0$$
$$(x + 5)(x + 5) = 0$$
$$x = -5$$

3 No real solution (cannot be factorised):

$$x^2 - 2x + 7 = 0$$

 ISBN: 9780170416009

Solve the following equations.

1 $x^2 + 6x + 8 = 0$

2 $x^2 - 7x + 10 = 0$

3 $x^2 - 4x - 21 = 0$

4 $x^2 - 6x = 0$

5 $x^2 + x - 12 = 0$

6 $x^2 - 49 = 0$

7 $4x^2 - 25 = 0$

8 $2x^2 - 8x - 42 = 0$

9 $2x^2 + 5x + 3 = 0$

10 $10x^2 + 13x - 3 = 0$

11 $22x - 6 + 8x^2 = 0$

12 $23x - 20x^2 - 6 = 0$

ISBN: 9780170416009

2 Using the quadratic formula

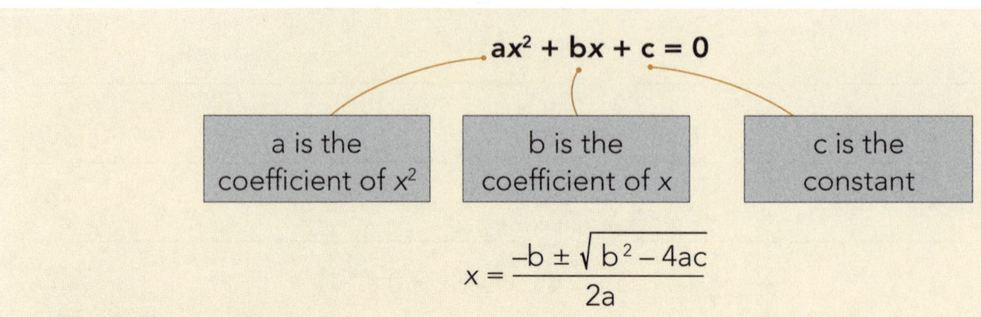

$$x = \frac{-b \pm \sqrt{b^2 - 4ac}}{2a}$$

Examples:

1 $x^2 + 5x + 6 = 0$

$a = 1 \quad b = 5 \quad c = 6$

$$x = \frac{-5 \pm \sqrt{5^2 - 4 \times 1 \times 6}}{2 \times 1}$$

$$x = \frac{-5 \pm \sqrt{1}}{2}$$

$x = -2$ or $x = -3$

2 $2x^2 + 9x + 3 = 0$

$a = 2 \quad b = 9 \quad c = 3$

$$x = \frac{-9 \pm \sqrt{9^2 - 4 \times 2 \times 3}}{2 \times 2}$$

$$x = \frac{-9 \pm \sqrt{57}}{4}$$

$x = -0.3625$ or $x = -4.1375$

3 $4x^2 - 12x + 9 = 0$

$a = 4 \quad b = -12 \quad c = 9$

$$x = \frac{-(-12) \pm \sqrt{(-12)^2 - 4 \times 4 \times 9}}{2 \times 4}$$

$$x = \frac{12 \pm \sqrt{0}}{8}$$

$x = 1.5$

One solution only

4 $x(x + 5) = 14$

$x^2 + 5x = 14$

$x^2 + 5x - 14 = 0$

Expand and simplify first

$a = 1 \quad b = 5 \quad c = -14$

$$x = \frac{-5 \pm \sqrt{5^2 - 4 \times 1 \times (-14)}}{2 \times 1}$$

$$x = \frac{-5 \pm \sqrt{81}}{2}$$

$x = 2$ or $x = -7$

Solve the following equations.

1 $x^2 + 6x + 8 = 0$

2 $x^2 - 7x + 10 = 0$

ISBN: 9780170416009

3 $x^2 - 4x - 21 = 0$

4 $x^2 - 6x = 0$

5 $x^2 + x - 12 = 0$

6 $x^2 - 49 = 0$

7 $3x^2 - 5x - 8 = 0$

8 $4x^2 + 5x = 11$

9 $1 - 7x + x^2 = 0$

10 $3x^2 - 5x = 13$

11 $9 + x^2 = 7x$

12 $7x = 4 + x^2$

ISBN: 9780170416009

3 On a calculator

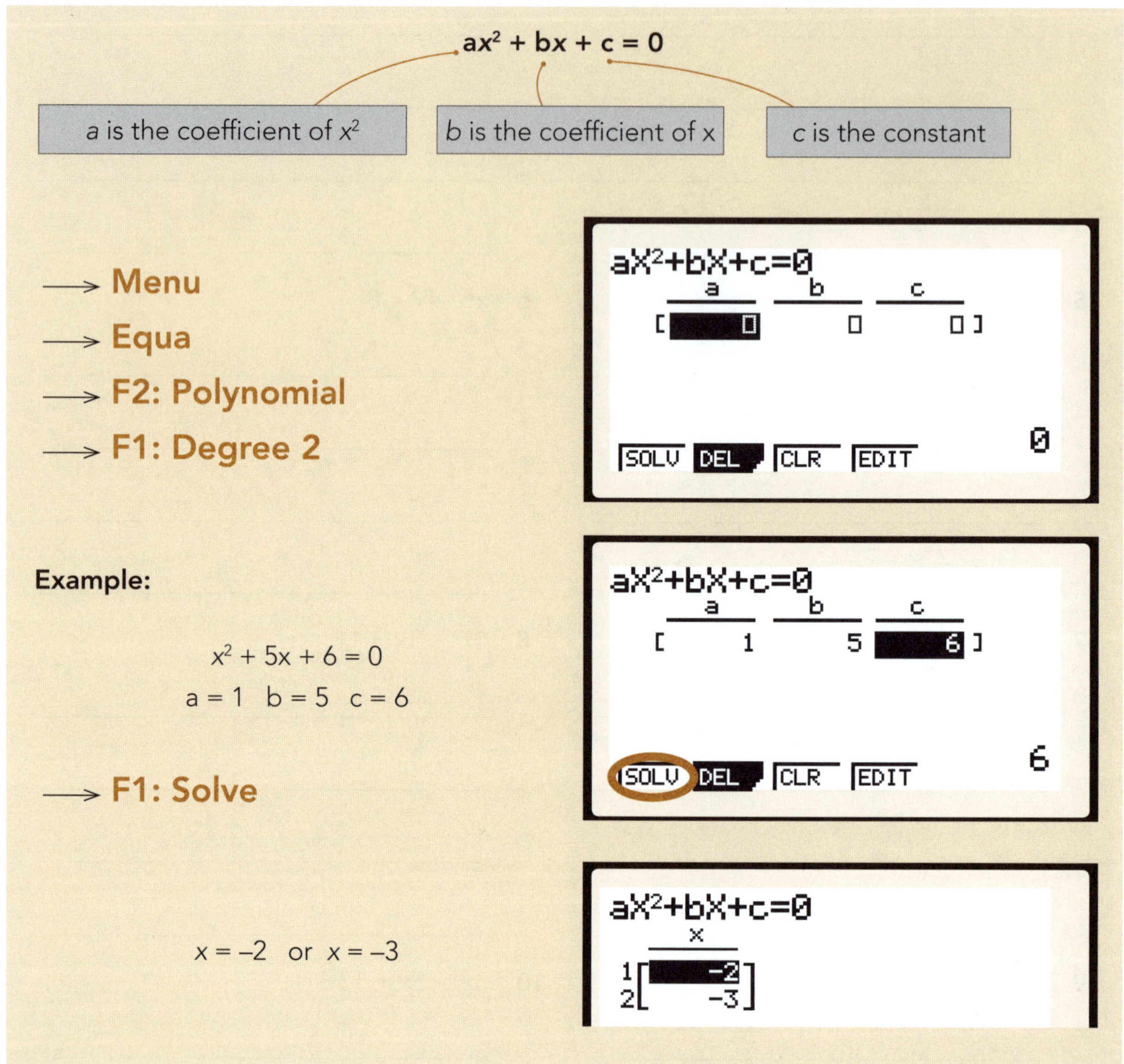

Solve the following using your graphics calculator. Compare your answers with the previous exercise.

1 $x^2 + 6x + 8 = 0$ ________________

2 $x^2 - 7x + 10 = 0$ ________________

3 $x^2 - 4x - 21 = 0$ ________________

4 $x^2 - 6x = 0$ ________________

5 $x^2 + x - 12 = 0$ ________________

6 $x^2 - 49 = 0$ ________________

7 $3x^2 - 5x - 8 = 0$ ________________

8 $4x^2 + 5x - 11 = 0$ ________________

9 $1 - 7x + x^2 = 0$ ________________

10 $3x^2 - 5x = 13$ ________________

11 $9 - 7x + x^2 = 0$ ________________

12 $-x^2 + 7x = 4$ ________________

  ISBN: 9780170416009

Finding how many solutions exist

- Quadratic equations have a maximum of two solutions, or points where the parabola crosses the x-axis. These solutions are also known as **roots**.
- We use the term 'real' roots, because at Level 3 you will learn about imaginary or unreal roots.
- You can tell how many roots there are by the value of $b^2 - 4ac$ in the quadratic formula. This is known as the **discriminant (Δ)**.
- There are three possibilities for the number of real roots:

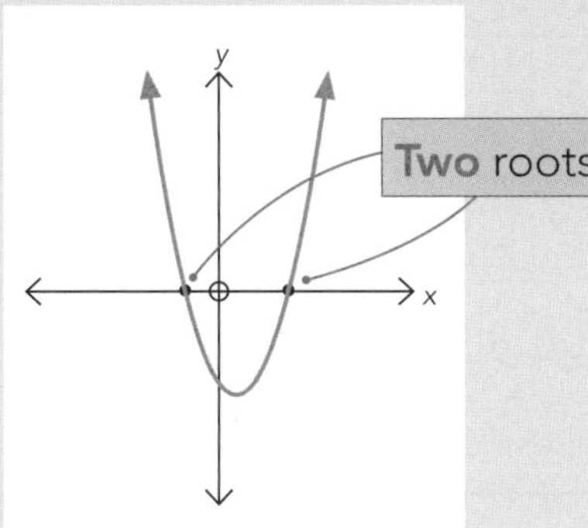

The discriminant is positive:

$$\Delta = b^2 - 4ac \; \mathbf{> 0}$$

$$\text{So } x = \frac{-b + \sqrt{\text{positive number}}}{2a}$$

$$\text{or } x = \frac{-b - \sqrt{\text{positive number}}}{2a}$$

So there are two real distinct roots.

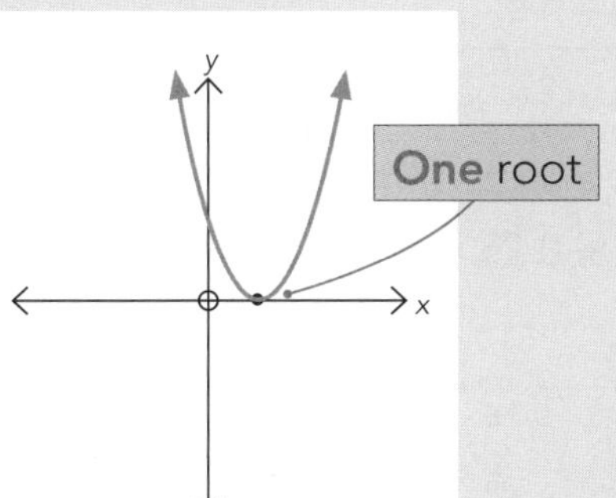

The discriminant is 0:

$$\Delta = b^2 - 4ac \; \mathbf{= 0}$$

$$\text{So} \quad x = \frac{-b \pm \sqrt{0}}{4ac} = \frac{-b}{4ac}$$

So there is one real root.
(This could be described as two identical roots.)

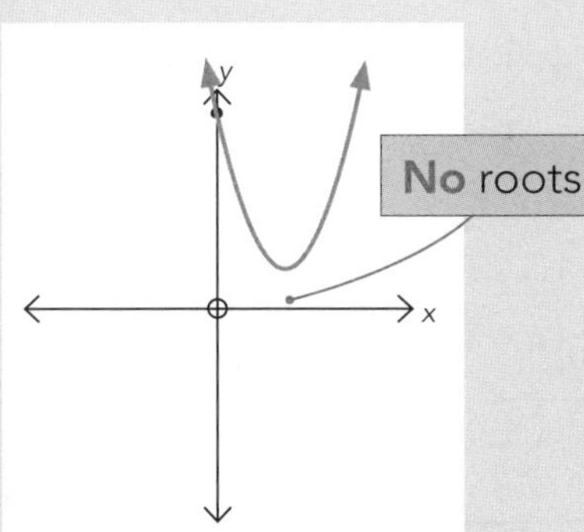

The discriminant is negative:

$$\Delta = b^2 - 4ac \; \mathbf{< 0}$$

But you cannot find $\sqrt{\text{negative number}}$

So there are no real roots.

Example: Calculate the value of the discriminant for $10x^2 - x - 3 = 0$, and use it to determine how many roots it has.

$$\begin{aligned} \Delta = b^2 - 4ac &= (-1)^2 - 4 \times 10 \times (-3) \\ &= 1 + 120 \\ &= +121 \end{aligned}$$

∴ the discriminant is positive, so there are two real roots.

Calculate the value of the discriminant and state the number of real roots.

1 $2x^2 + x - 10 = 0$

2 $4x^2 - 4x + 1 = 0$

3 $4x^2 - 3x + 1 = 0$

4 $x^2 - 2x + 0.25 = 0$

5 $7x^2 + 11x + 4 = 0$

6 $7x^2 + 5x + 2 = 0$

7 $36x^2 - 6x + 0.25 = 0$

8 $x^2 - x + 0.25 = 0$

9 $3 - 2x + x^2 = 0$

10 $3x^2 - 5x - 6 = 0$

11 $9 - 5x + x^2 = 0$

12 $x^2 - 7x + 12.5 = 0$

ISBN: 9780170416009

Sometimes you might need to rearrange the equation first.

Examples:

1 Calculate the value of the discriminant and state the number of real roots for the equation $5x^2 = 3x - 6$.

Step 1: Reorganise into $ax^2 + bx + c = 0$ form. $5x^2 - 3x + 6 = 0$

Step 2: Calculate the discriminant.

$$\begin{aligned} b^2 - 4ac &= (-3)^2 - 4 \times 5 \times 6 \\ &= 9 - 120 \\ &= -111 \end{aligned}$$

Negative discriminant.

$\therefore$ $5x^2 = 3x - 6$ has no real roots

2 Calculate the value of the discriminant and state the number of real roots for the equation $12x = 4x^2 + 9$.

Step 1: Reorganise into $ax^2 + bx + c = 0$ form. $4x^2 - 12x + 9 = 0$

Step 2: Calculate the discriminant.

$$\begin{aligned} b^2 - 4ac &= (-12)^2 - 4 \times 4 \times 9 \\ &= 144 - 144 \\ &= 0 \end{aligned}$$

Discriminant = 0.

$\therefore$ $12x = 4x^2 + 9$ has one real root

Calculate the value of the discriminant and state the number of real roots.

13 $3x^2 = 20 - 13x$

14 $3x^2 = 2 - 5x$

15 $x^2 + 12x = 9 + 5x^2$

16 $(5x + 1)^2 = -1$

17 $5x^2 + 11x - 4 = 17x - 4x^2 - 5$

18 $11x^2 - 17 = 60x - 4x^2$

Simultaneous equations

- You will need to find the point(s) where a straight line and a curve meet.
- The curves that you need to be familiar with are parabolas, circles and hyperbolas.
- In each case they may not meet at all, or they may meet at one or two points.
- Solving the equations of the straight line and the curve simultaneously will produce a quadratic equation.
- Solving it will tell you **where** they meet.
- Finding its discriminant will tell you the **number of points** at which they meet.

Line and parabola

Here are the three possibilities for the relationship between a line and a parabola.

1 They meet at two points

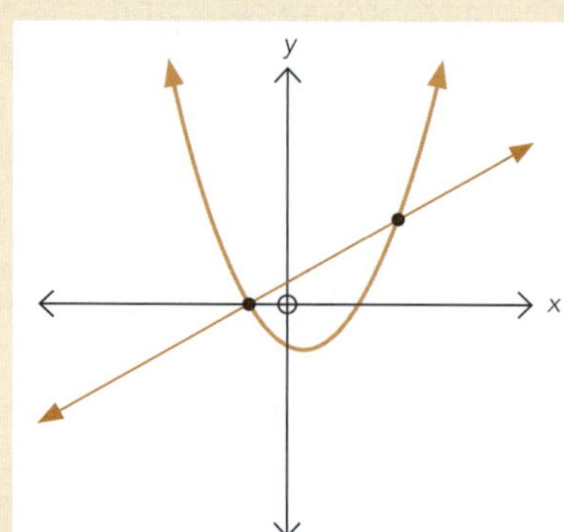

Parabola: $y = x^2 - x - 2$ ①
Line: $y = x + 1$ ②

Solving these:

Substitute for y in ①: $x + 1 = x^2 - x - 2$

Reorganise → 0 on one side: $x^2 - 2x - 3 = 0$

Solve: $(x + 1)(x - 3) = 0$

$\therefore x = -1$ or 3

Find the points at which they meet:

Where $x = -1$:

Substitute for x in ②:

$y = x + 1$
$= (-1) + 1$
$= 0$

$\therefore$ They meet at $(-1, 0)$

Select the equation that is easiest — definitely the line.

Where $x = 3$:

Substitute for x in ②:

$y = x + 1$
$= (3) + 1$
$= 4$

$\therefore$ They meet at $(3, 4)$

$\therefore$ The parabola $y = x^2 - x - 2$ and the line $y = x + 1$ meet at two points: $(-1, 0)$ and $(3, 4)$.

  ISBN: 9780170416009

2 They meet at one point

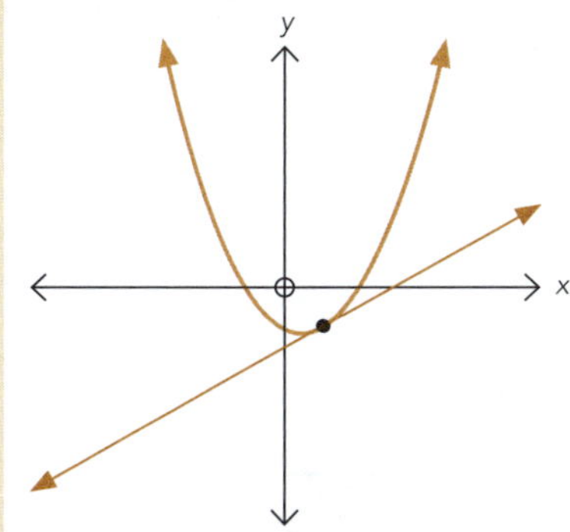

Parabola: $y = x^2 - x - 2$ ①
Line: $y = x - 3$ ②

Solving these:

Substitute for y in ①: $x - 3 = x^2 - x - 2$

Reorganise → 0 on one side: $x^2 - 2x + 1 = 0$

Solve: $(x - 1)^2 = 0$

$\therefore x = 1$

Find the point at which they meet:

Where $x = 1$:

Substitute for x in ②:

$y = x - 3$
$= (1) - 3$
$= -2$

$\therefore$ They meet at $(1, -2)$

Select the equation that is easiest.

$\therefore$ The parabola $y = x^2 - x - 2$ and the line $y = x - 3$ meet at one point: $(1, -2)$.

3 They do not meet

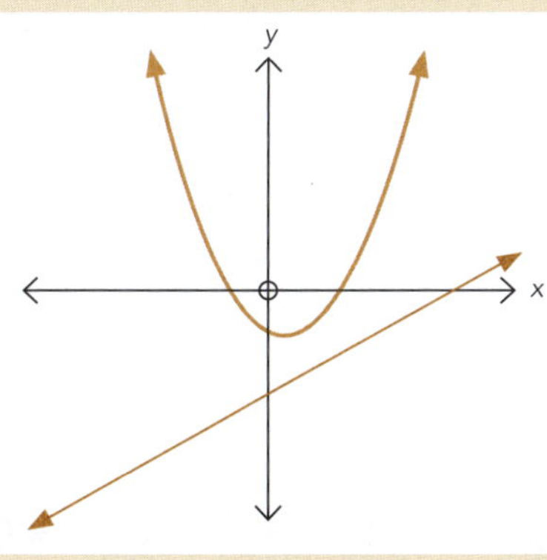

Parabola: $y = x^2 - x - 2$ ①
Line: $y = x - 5$ ②

Solving these:

Substitute for y in ①: $x - 5 = x^2 - x - 2$

Reorganise → 0 on one side: $x^2 - 2x + 3 = 0$

Solve: This does not factorise, so use the formula:

$$x = \frac{-(-2) \pm \sqrt{(-2)^2 - 4 \times 1 \times 3}}{2 \times 1}$$

$$= \frac{2 \pm \sqrt{-8}}{2}$$

Δ is **negative** → no solutions.

$\therefore$ The parabola $y = x^2 - x - 2$ and the line $y = x - 5$ never meet.

For the following equations, use the discriminant to determine the number of possible solutions, and then find the coordinates of any point(s) where the line and parabola meet.

1 $y = x^2 + 2$ and $y = 4 - x$

2 $y = 2x + 3$ and $y = (x + 2)^2$

3 $y = 2x$ and $y = (x + 3)(x - 2)$

4 $y = (x - 1)^2 + 4$ and $2y = x + 4$

5 $y = -2x + 2$ and $y + x^2 = 4x - 3$

6 $x^2 + y + 6x + 10 = 0$ and $y + 4x + 9 = 0$

 ISBN: 9780170416009

7 $y + (x - 8)^2 = 40$ and $y = 5x + 7$

8 $y = (x + 5)(x - 2) + 3$ and $y = 3x + 9$

9 $y + 15x = x^2 + 66$ and $y + 3x = 55$

10 $y = 45 - (x - 5)(x - 12)$ and $y + 4x = 75$

11 $x^2 = 21x + y - 115$ and $15x = 106 - y$

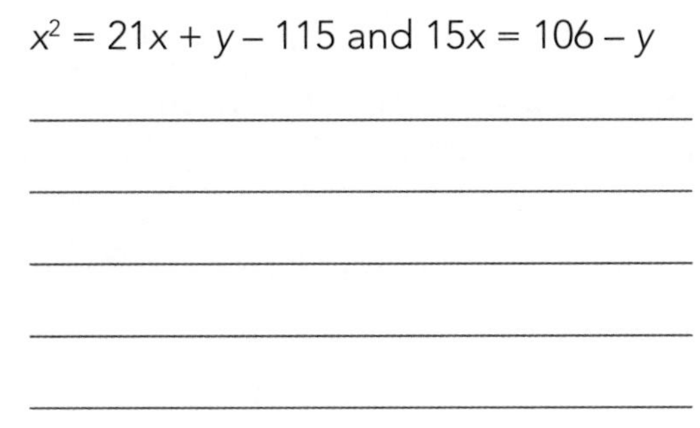

12 $y = -2(x - 3)(x - 25) - 47$ and $y = 195$

ISBN: 9780170416009

Line and circle

As with parabolas, these may not meet at all, or they may meet at one or two points.

Here are the three possibilities for the relationship between a line and a circle.

1 They meet at two points

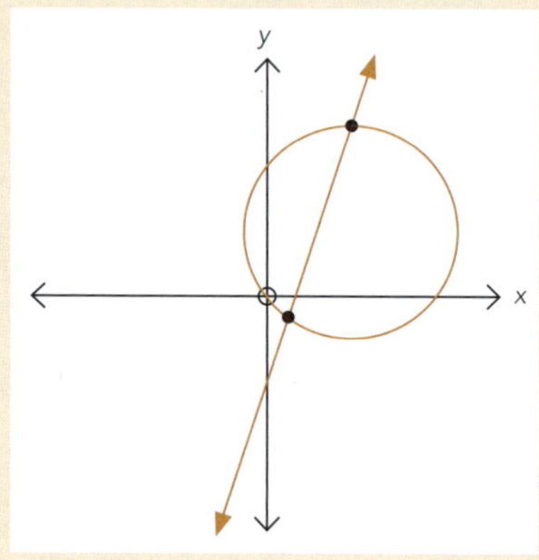

Circle: $(x - 4)^2 + (y - 3)^2 = 25$ ①
Line: $y = 3x - 4$ ②

Solving these:

Substitute for y in ①: $(x - 4)^2 + ((3x - 4) - 3)^2 = 25$

Simplify: $(x - 4)^2 + (3x - 7)^2 = 25$

Expand brackets: $x^2 - 8x + 16 + 9x^2 - 42x + 49 = 25$

Reorganise → 0 on one side: $10x^2 - 50x + 40 = 0$

Divide by 10: $x^2 - 5x + 4 = 0$

Solve: $(x - 1)(x - 4) = 0$

$\therefore$ **x = 1 or 4**

Select the equation which is easiest – definitely the line.

Find the points at which they meet:

Where x = 1:

Substitute for x in ②:
$y = 3x - 4$
$= 3(1) - 4$
$= -1$
$\therefore$ They meet at (1, –1)

Where x = 4:

Substitute for x in ②:
$y = 3x - 4$
$= 3(4) - 4$
$= 8$
$\therefore$ They meet at (4, 8)

$\therefore$ **The circle $(x - 4)^2 + (y - 3)^2 = 25$ and the line $y = 3x - 4$ meet at two points: (1, –1) and (4, 8).**

ISBN: 9780170416009

2 They meet at one point

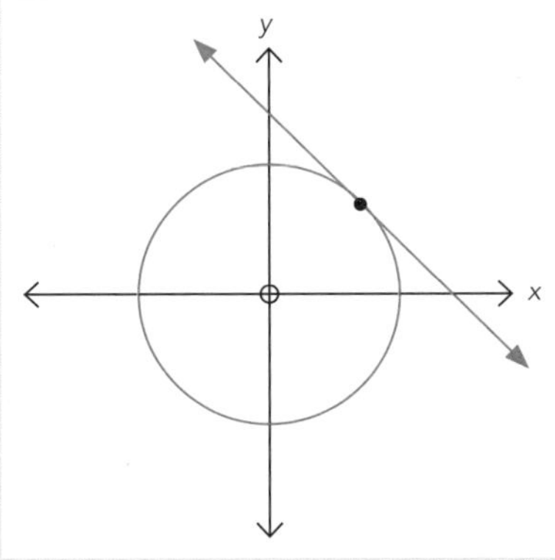

Circle: $x^2 + y^2 = 32$ ①
Line: $y = 8 - x$ ②

Solving these:

Substitute for y in ①:	$x^2 + (8 - x)^2 = 32$
Expand brackets:	$x^2 + (64 - 16x + x^2) = 32$
Reorganise → 0 on one side:	$2x^2 - 16x + 32 = 0$
Solve:	$2(x - 4)(x - 4) = 0$
	$\therefore \mathbf{x = 4}$

Find the point at which they meet:
Where x = 4:

Substitute for x in ②:

$$\begin{aligned} y &= 8 - x \\ &= 8 - 4 \\ &= 4 \end{aligned}$$

∴ They meet at (4, 4)

∴ The circle $x^2 + y^2 = 32$ and the line $y = 8 - x$ meet at one point: (4, 4).

3 They do not meet

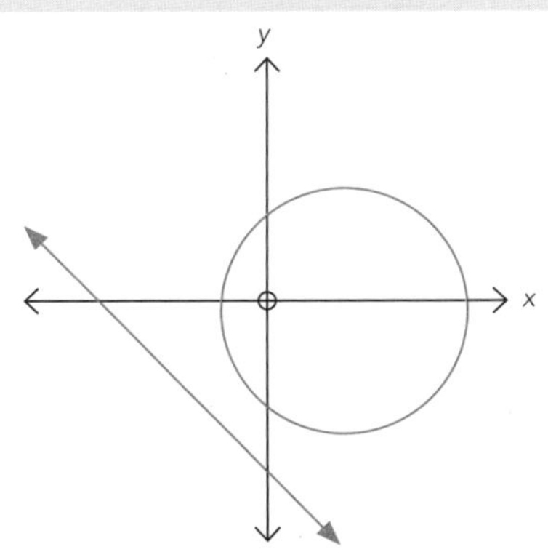

Circle: $x(x - 7) + (y - 4)(y + 5) = 0$ ①
Line: $y = -x - 8$ ②

Solving these:

Substitute for y in ①:	$x(x - 7) + ((-x - 8) - 4)((-x - 8) + 5) = 0$
Simplify:	$x^2 - 7x + (-x - 12)(-x - 3) = 0$
Expand brackets:	$x^2 - 7x + x^2 + 15x + 36 = 0$
Reorganise:	$2x^2 + 8x + 36 = 0$
Divide by 2:	$x^2 + 4x + 18 = 0$

Solve: This does not factorise, so use the formula:

$$x = \frac{-(4) \pm \sqrt{(4)^2 - 4 \times 1 \times 18}}{2 \times 1}$$

$$= \frac{-4 \pm \sqrt{-56}}{2}$$

Δ is negative ⇒ no solutions.

∴ The circle $x(x - 7) + (y - 4)(y + 5) = 0$ and the line $y = -x - 8$ never meet.

ISBN: 9780170416009

For the following equations, use the discriminant to determine the number of possible solutions, and then find the coordinates of any point(s) where the line and circle meet.

1 $x^2 + y^2 = 25$ and $y = x - 1$

2 $x^2 + y^2 = 29$ and $y = x - 7$

3 $x^2 + y^2 = 50$ and $y = 6 - x$

4 $x^2 + y^2 = 72$ and $y = 12 - x$

5 $x^2 + y^2 = 45$ and $x + y + 10 = 0$

6 $x^2 + y^2 = 61$ and $y = 6$

 ISBN: 9780170416009

7 $x(x-5)+y(y+3)=50$ and $y=2x+11$

8 $x^2+y(y+2)=40$ and $5y=4x-5$

9 $x(x-4)+y^2=113$ and $y=5-x$

10 $x^2+y^2=169$ and $y=-\frac{5}{12}x$

11 $x^2+(y+11)^2=306$ and $y=2x+29$

12 $(x+5)^2+(y-2)^2=148$ and $y=46-6x$

ISBN: 9780170416009

Line and hyperbola

As with parabolas and circles, these may not meet at all, or they may meet at one or two points.

Here are the three possibilities for the relationship between a line and a hyperbola.

1 They meet at two points

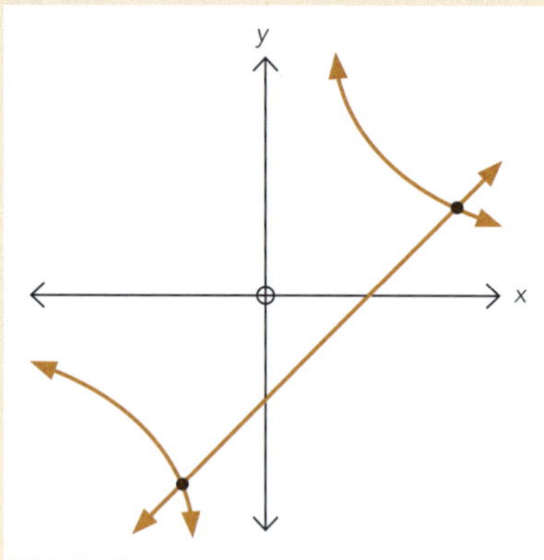

Hyperbola: $xy = 36$ ①
Line: $y = x - 5$ ②

Solving these:

Substitute for y in ①: $x(x - 5) = 36$

Expand bracket: $x^2 - 5x - 36 = 0$

Solve: $(x - 9)(x + 4) = 0$

$\therefore$ **$x = 9$ or -4**

Find the points at which they meet:

Where $x = 9$:

Substitute for x in ②: $y = 9 - 5$
$= 4$
$\therefore$ They meet at (9, 4)

Where $x = -4$:

Substitute for x in ②: $y = -4 - 5$
$= -9$
$\therefore$ They meet at (–4, –9)

$\therefore$ **The hyperbola $xy = 36$ and the line $y = x - 5$ meet at two points: (9, 4) and (–4, –9).**

Note: It is also possible to have two solutions when a line crosses a hyperbola like this:

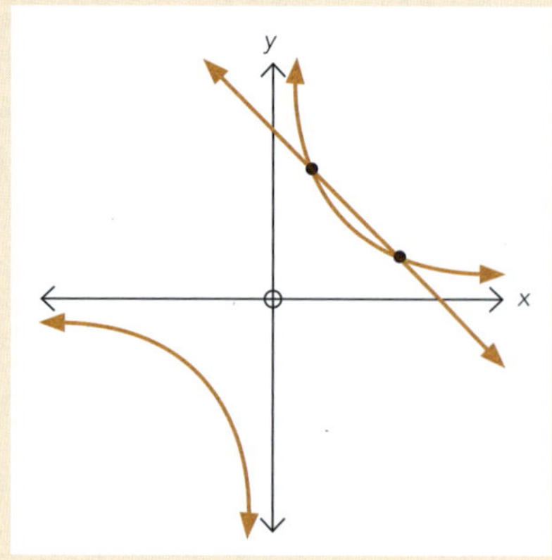

Hyperbola: $xy = 12$ ①
Line: $y = -x + 8$ ②

These meet at (2, 6) and (6, 2).

ISBN: 9780170416009

2 They meet at one point

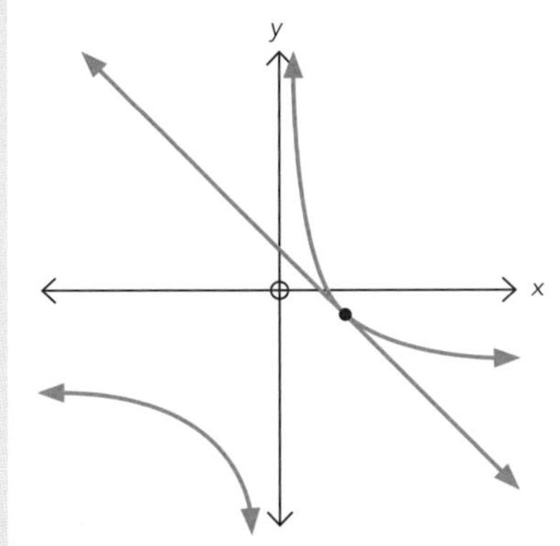

Hyperbola: $\mathbf{x(y + 4) = 9}$ ①
Line: $\mathbf{y = 2 - x}$ ②

Solving these:

Substitute for y in ①:	$x((2 - x) + 4) = 9$
Simplify:	$x(6 - x) = 9$
Expand bracket:	$6x - x^2 = 9$
Reorganise → 0 on one side:	$x^2 - 6x + 9 = 0$
Solve:	$(x - 3)(x - 3) = 0$
	$\therefore \mathbf{x = 3}$

Find the point at which they meet:
Where x = 3:

Substitute for x in ②: $y = 2 - 3$
$= -1$
$\therefore$ They meet at $(3, -1)$

$\therefore$ **The hyperbola $x(y + 4) = 9$ and the line $y = 2 - x$ meet at one point: $(3, -1)$.**

3 They do not meet

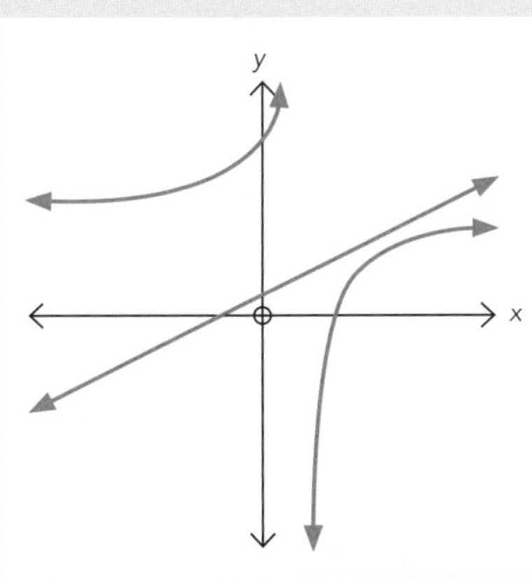

Hyperbola: $\mathbf{(2 - x)(y - 5) = 7}$ ①
Line: $\mathbf{y = \frac{1}{2}x + 1}$ ②

Solving these:

Substitute for y in ①:	$(2 - x)((\frac{1}{2}x + 1) - 5) = 7$
Simplify:	$(2 - x)(\frac{1}{2}x - 4) = 7$
Expand brackets:	$x - 8 - \frac{1}{2}x^2 + 4x = 7$
Reorganise:	$\frac{1}{2}x^2 - 5x + 15 = 0$
Multiply by 2:	$x^2 - 10x + 30 = 0$

Solve: This does not factorise, so use the formula:

$$x = \frac{-(-10) \pm \sqrt{(-10)^2 - 4 \times 1 \times 30}}{2 \times 1}$$

$$= \frac{10 \pm \sqrt{-20}}{2}$$

Δ is **negative** ⇒ no solutions.

$\therefore$ **The hyperbola $(2 - x)(y - 5) = 7$ and the line $y = \frac{1}{2}x + 1$ never meet.**

For the following equations, use the discriminant to determine the number of possible solutions, and then find the coordinates of any point(s) where the line and circle meet.

1 $xy = 16$ and $y = x$

2 $xy = 12$ and $y = x + 4$

3 $xy = -25$ and $y = x + 10$

4 $y = \frac{36}{x}$ and $y = 4x$

5 $y = -\frac{10}{x}$ and $y = 2x + 8$

6 $x(y - 5) = 6$ and $y = x + 4$

ISBN: 9780170416009

7 $y = \dfrac{10}{x + 3}$ and $y = 5x + 10$

8 $xy - 7x = 9$ and $y = 13 - x$

9 $xy - 9y - 13 = 0$ and $2x + y - 27 = 0$

10 $x - 10 = \dfrac{18}{y - 3}$ and $y = \dfrac{3}{2}x - 6$

11 $(x + 1)(y - 8) = 4$ and $y = 3 - x$

12 $x = \dfrac{24}{y - 12}$ and $3y = x + 11$

ISBN: 9780170416009

Finding unknown values, given the number of solutions

- You may need to calculate the value of one of the coefficients or constants in the equation for a straight line or curve.
- You can do this if you know the number of solutions to the quadratic equation formed when these are solved simultaneously.
- The number of solutions to a system determines whether the discriminant ($\Delta = b^2 - 4ac$) is negative, 0 or positive.

Example: Consider the simultaneous equations $y = -2(x - 3)(x - 4) + 5$ and $y = px - 1$. Give values of p for which there are one solution, no solutions or two solutions.

Step 1: Expand and simplify $y = -2(x - 3)(x - 4) + 5$:

$$y = -2(x^2 - 7x + 12) + 5$$
$$= -2x^2 + 14x - 19$$

Step 2: Solve $y = -2x^2 + 14x - 19$ and $y = px - 1$ simultaneously:

$$-2x^2 + 14x - 19 = px - 1$$
$$px - 1 + 2x^2 - 14x + 19 = 0$$
$$2x^2 + (p - 14)x + 18 = 0$$

Step 3: Use the discriminant, $\Delta = b^2 - 4ac$, to find values of p that give one solution, no solutions or two solutions:

Step 3a: **One solution ⇒** $\mathbf{b^2 - 4ac = 0}$

$$(p - 14)^2 - 4 \times 2 \times 18 = 0$$
$$p^2 - 28p + 196 - 144 = 0$$
$$p^2 - 28p + 52 = 0$$
$$(p - 2)(p - 26) = 0$$
$$\therefore p = 2 \text{ or } 26$$

∴ There is one solution to the equations:

$y = -2(x - 3)(x - 4) + 5$ and $y = 2x - 1$

or $y = -2(x - 3)(x - 4) + 5$ and $y = 26x - 1$

This means that $y = 2x - 1$ and $y = 26x - 1$ are both tangents to the parabola $y = -2(x - 3)(x - 4) + 5$.

 ISBN: 9780170416009

Graph of this situation:

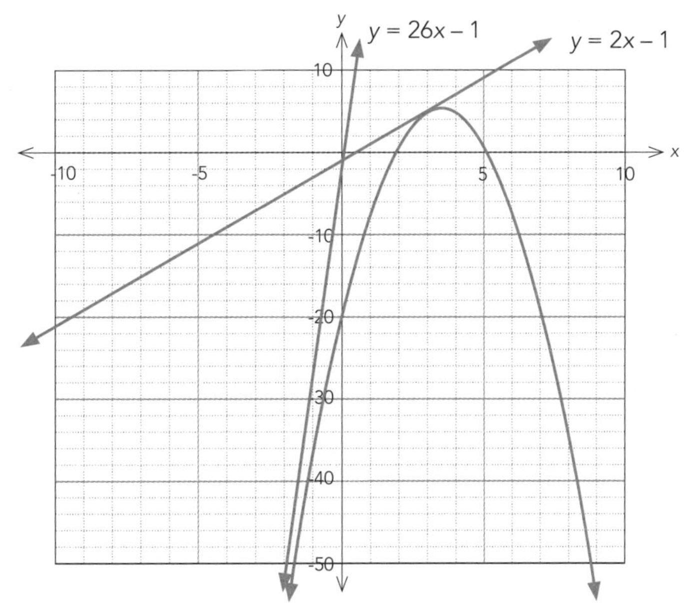

Step 3b: **No solutions ⇒** $\mathbf{b^2 - 4ac < 0}$

$$p^2 - 28p + 52 < 0$$
$$(p - 2)(p - 26) < 0$$
$$\therefore 2 < p < 26$$

e.g. p = 10:

$$b^2 - 4ac = (p - 2)(p - 26)$$
$$= (10 - 2)(10 - 26)$$
$$= -128$$

∴ If $2 < p < 26$, then $b^2 - 4ac < 0 \Rightarrow$ There are no solutions to the equations $y = -2(x - 3)(x - 4) + 5$ and $y = px - 1$.

This means that if 2 < p < 26, then the line $y = px - 1$ never crosses the parabola $y = -2(x - 3)(x - 4) + 5$.

Step 3c: **Two solutions ⇒** $\mathbf{b^2 - 4ac > 0}$

$$p^2 - 28p + 52 > 0$$
$$(p - 2)(p - 26) > 0$$
$$\therefore p < 2 \text{ or } p > 26$$

e.g. p = 0:

$$b^2 - 4ac = (p - 2)(p - 26)$$
$$= (0 - 2)(0 - 26)$$
$$= 52$$

∴ If $p < 2$ or $p > 26$, then $b^2 - 4ac > 0 \rightarrow$ There are two solutions to the equations $y = -2(x - 3)(x - 4) + 5$ and $y = px - 1$.

This means that if p < 2 or p > 26, then the line $y = px - 1$ cuts the parabola $y = -2(x - 3)(x - 4) + 5$ in two places.

Answer the following questions.

1 **a** Consider the equations $xy = 49$ and $y = p - x$. Find value(s) of p so that $y = p - x$ forms a tangent to the hyperbola.

b Find the coordinates of the points where the tangents touch the hyperbola.

c For what values of p are there no solutions to the equations $xy = 49$ and $y = p - x$? Show your reasoning.

2 **a** Consider the equations $x^2 + y^2 = p$ and $y = 10 - x$. Find value(s) of p so there is only one solution to this system of equations.

b Solve the equations simultaneously.

c Explain the geometrical significance of your answers to **a** and **b**.

d For what values of p are there two solutions to the equations $x^2 + y^2 = p$ and $y = 10 - x$? Show your reasoning.

ISBN: 9780170416009

3 **a** Consider the equations $y = -(x - 6)^2 + 7$ and $y = 4x + p$. Find value(s) of p so that $y = 4x + p$ forms a tangent to the parabola.

b Where does the tangent touch the parabola?

c For what values of p does the line cut the parabola in two places?

4 **a** Consider the equations $y = 0.5(x - 1)(x - 4)$ and $y = px - 2.5$. Find value(s) of p so that there is only one solution to this system of equations.

b Solve this system of equations.

c Explain the geometrical significance of your answers to **a** and **b**.

d For what values of p are there no solutions to the equations $y = 0.5(x - 1)(x - 4)$ and $y = px - 2.5$? Show your reasoning.

ISBN: 9780170416009

Mixing it up, with applications

Answer the following.

1 The following equations have been used to create the face shown below.

a Match the equations to the components of the face.

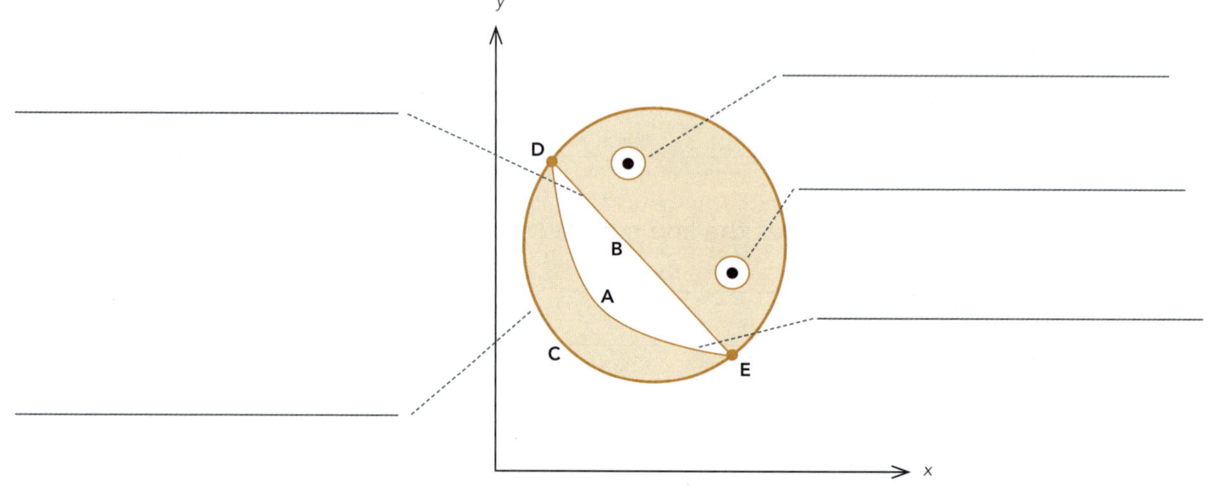

$$(x - 6)^2 + (y - 8)^2 = 25$$
$$(x - 1)(y - 3) = 8$$
$$y = -x + 13$$
$$(x - 5)^2 + (y - 11)^2 = 0.36$$
$$(x - 9)^2 + (y - 7)^2 = 0.36$$

b Solve equations A and B in order to find the coordinates of points D and E.

c Solve equations B and C in order to confirm that your answer to **b** was correct.

  ISBN: 9780170416009

2 Will, Sefa and Jack have each earned \$60 to spend while on a 10-day holiday. They each spend the money at different rates, and two of them do not spend it all. The following equations model the rates at which they spent it, where x represents the number of days since the start of the holiday, and y represents the amount each has left.

- Will $y = 0.6(x - 10)^2$
- Sefa $(x + 5)y = 300$
- Jack $y = 60 - 5x$

a Calculate how much each has after five days.

b Who has the most at the end of the holiday?

c How much does Jack spend each day? Explain how you know this.

d On which day did Sefa and Jack have the same amount of money left, and how much did they both have?

e Make one change to the equation which models Jack's spending so that he and Sefa both have the same amount at the end of the holiday.

ISBN: 9780170416009

3 A group of up to 12 friends is going away for the weekend. There are two baches available for hire — Cosy Cottage and Ben's Bach. Both have enough beds for 12 people.

a Ben's Bach costs \$120 per night for one person, \$110 per night each for two people, \$100 per night each for three people, etc.
Write an equation to model this situation. Let *y* represent the cost per person per night, and *x* represent the number of friends who sleep there.

b Cosy Cottage costs \$360 per night, regardless of how many people stay there. If the cost is shared evenly, this can be modelled by the equation $xy = 360$.
Solve the two equations simultaneously in order to find the number of friends for which both baches cost the same, and the cost per night for each friend.

c Make a recommendation for which bach they should hire depending on how many of them go for the weekend.

d They discover that Ben is a cousin of one of the friends. He will let them have the bach at 'mate's rates'. This will cost them \$110 per night for one person, \$100 per night each for two people, \$90 per night each for three people, etc.
Investigate how this would change your answers to **b** and **c**.

ISBN: 9780170416009

4 Max is entering a Rube Goldberg 'Smash the egg' competition.
(If you haven't seen one of these, watch **https://www.youtube.com/watch?v=yNXh3qZ8rzQ** and **https://www.youtube.com/watch?v=fscReJ9j51E**.)
This involves rolling a large ball bearing down a series of slopes. The diagram shows part of his design.

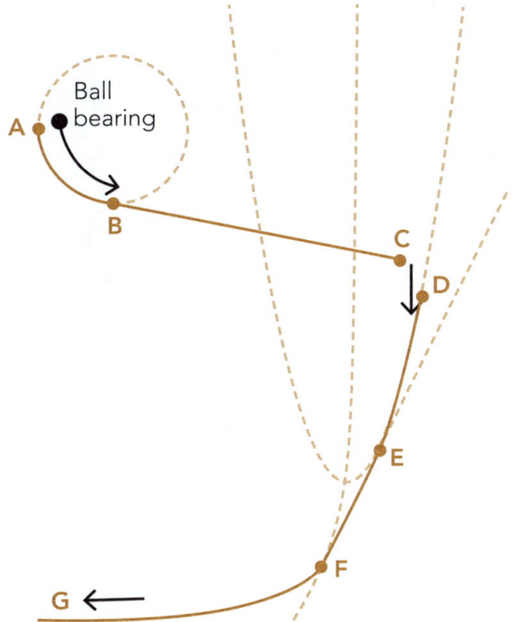

A → B	Quarter circle
B → C	Straight line
C → D	Gap
D → E	Part of a parabola
E → F	Tangent to the parabola
F → G	Part of a hyperbola

Other information:

- Point B is the lowest point on the circle.
- The coordinates of point C are (25, 25).
- Point D lies on the line $x = 26$.
- The gradient of EF is 2.
- G is located at the lowest possible point.

Some equations used for different sections of his design area:

$$(x - 22)y = -12$$

$$(x - 5)^2 + (y - 34)^2 = 25$$

$$y = \frac{1}{2}(x - 21)^2 + 10$$

Find the following, justifying all your answers.

a The equation of AB.

b The coordinates of A and B.

c The equation of BC.

d The equation of DE.

e The coordinates of D.

ISBN: 9780170416009

f The equation of CD.

g The equation of EF.

h The equation of FG.

i The coordinates of F.

ISBN: 9780170416009

5 A circular sign is to be attached to a building at points A and D. The equation of the circle is $(x - 10)^2 + (y - 10)^2 = 100$.

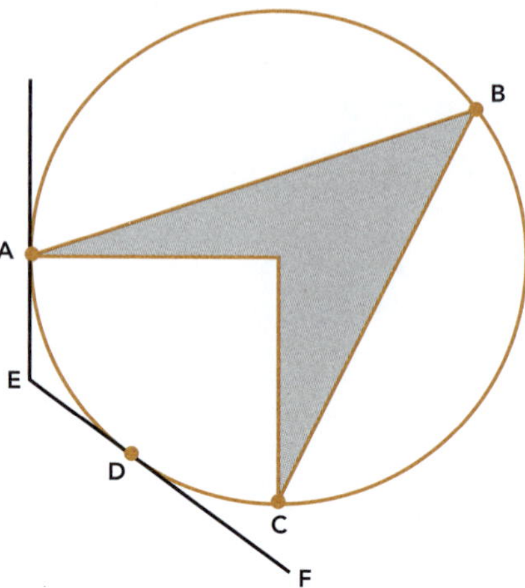

a If the equation of BC is $y = 2x - 20$, calculate the coordinates of points B and C.

b The coordinates of A are (0, 10). Calculate the equation of the line AB.

c Point E has the coordinates (0, 5). Find the equation of the line EF so that it forms a tangent to the circle.

ISBN: 9780170416009

6 Aroha, Brody and Clara are having a competition to see who can grow the tallest sunflower. The plants are 20 cm high when they begin, and the competition ends after 80 days. The relationship between the number of days (x) and the height of each sunflower (y) can be modelled by the equations below:

- Aroha $(x - 100)(10 - y) = 1000$
- Brody $y = \frac{6}{15}x + 20$
- Clara $y = \frac{1}{160}x^2 + 20$

a How high is each of their sunflowers after 20 days?

b Who won the competition and by how much?

c After how many days were Aroha's and Brody's sunflowers the same height? How high were they?

d Assume that the change in height of Brody's sunflower follows a straight line. Write an equation for the relationship between the number of days (x) and the height of his sunflower (y) so that the competition was a dead heat between all three competitors.

ISBN: 9780170416009

7 The diagram shows the end wall of a tent. A flexible pole forms the outer edge of the wall (CABD).

- Between A and B it takes the shape $y = -0.5(x-5)^2 + 8$.
- AC and BD are formed by tangents to the curve $y = -0.5(x-5)^2 + 8$.
- There are also two reinforced seams in the end wall: AF and BE. These are formed by straight lines which are parallel to BD and AC respectively.
- The equation of AC is $y = 2x$.

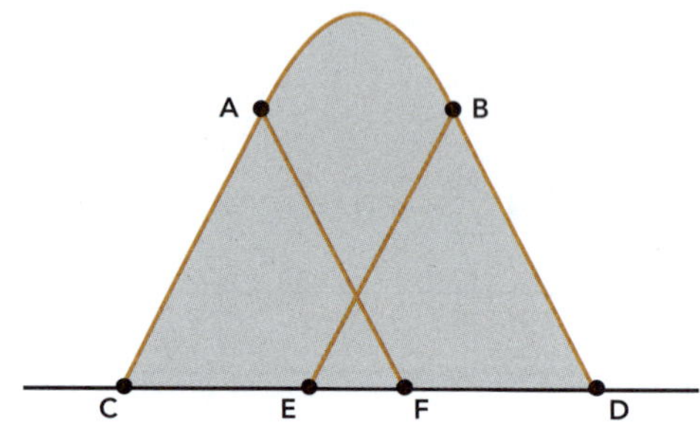

a Calculate the coordinates of point A.

____

____

____

b The coordinates of F are (6, 0). Calculate the equation of the reinforced line AF.

____

____

____

c The reinforced line EB is parallel with AC, and the coordinates of E are (4, 0). Find the equation of EB.

____

____

____

d The line BD is a tangent to the curved top of the tent, and it is parallel to the reinforced line AF. Use this information to help you find the equation for BD.

____

____

____

____

____

____

____

____

ISBN: 9780170416009

8 The cross-section of a tunnel is shown on the graph below. Each unit represents a measurement of one metre. The x-axis represents the tunnel floor.

- The tunnel's internal lining takes the shape of the parabola $y = -0.2(x - 1)(x - 15)$.
- The outer margin of the walls takes the shape of the parabola $y = -0.2x(x - 16)$.
- The ceiling in the tunnel is angled, and given by the line $y = 0.2x + 7$.

a Calculate the coordinates for the points where the ceiling meets the tunnel walls.

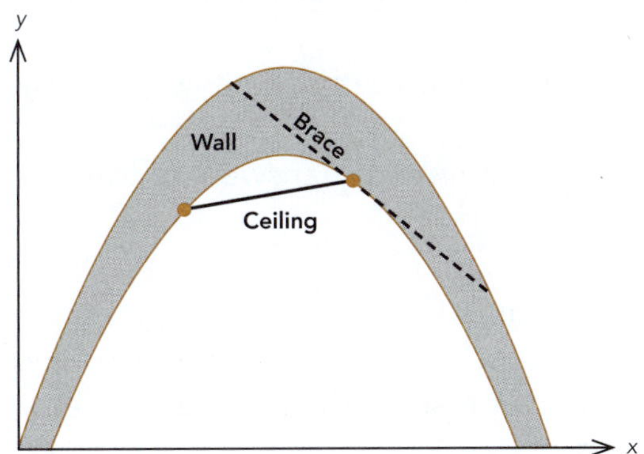

b A very large rectangular piece of machinery has to be moved through the tunnel. It is 8.4 m high and 3.5 m wide. Will it fit? Justify your answer.

c When the tunnel was being designed, a brace ($y = -1.2x + p$) was to be built into the tunnel wall. Find the value of p so that the brace forms a tangent to the inner wall of the tunnel.

Practice tasks

Practice task one

The student council sells melon slices and Juicies at three school events at the start of every year: the Year 9 welcome day, the gala sports day, and the swimming sports. They have some information from the previous year but would like to complete this so they can plan their sales for this year.

For each event, you need to find out how many melon slices and Juicies were sold, and at what prices.

Show all your reasoning, and link your answers to the context.

Year 9 welcome day

- They sold 350 items in total.
- The relationship between the number of melon slices and the number of Juicies was $x^2 + 2y = 25\,980$, where x represents the number of melon slices sold and y represents the number of Juicies sold.
- They charged 50c for melon slices.
- After all the melon slices and Juicies were sold, they had \$270.

 ISBN: 9780170416009

The gala sports day

- They sold melon slices for \$0.50 and Juicies for \$0.90.
- The relationship between the number of melon slices and the number of Juicies was $3xy + 10x = 15\,000$, where x represents the number of melon slices sold and y represents the number of Juicies sold.
- They sold fewer than 150 items all together.
- After all the melon slices and Juicies were sold, they had \$102.

ISBN: 9780170416009

The swimming sports

- They charged \$1 each for Juicies, but the price they charged for melon slices has been lost.
- The relationship between the number of melon slices and the number of Juicies was $100y = 10\,000 - x^2$, where x represents the number of melon slices sold and y represents the number of Juicies sold.
- After all the melon slices and Juicies were sold, they had \$109.
- There needs to be only one possibility for the price of a melon slice.

ISBN: 9780170416009

Practice task two

Part of a logo is shown below, along with the equations used to create it.

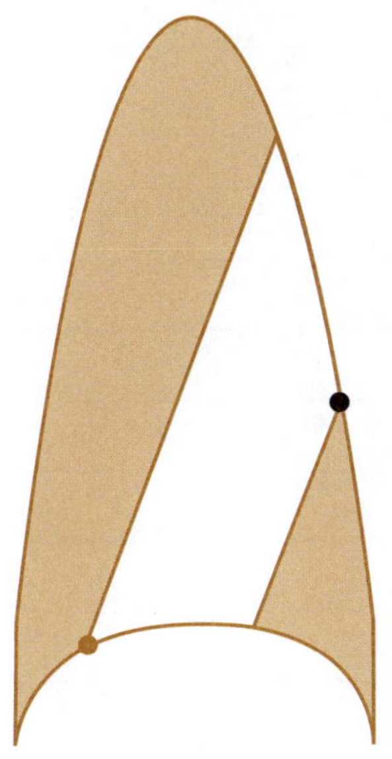

Equations for the design:

$y + x^2 + 34 = 16x$
$(x - 8)^2 + y^2 = 25$
$y = 4x - 16$
$y = 4x - 34$
$x = 3$
$x = 13$

Analyse the design following the steps below. Take care to justify all your choices.

Find the location of the black dot.

Find the location of the gold dot.

ISBN: 9780170416009

A new line is to be drawn. It must:

- be parallel to the other two diagonal lines, and
- form a tangent to the parabola.

Find the equation of this new line, and the point at which it touches the parabola.

 ISBN: 9780170416009

Practice task three

A farmer is going to fence a paddock, in order to have an enclosure for keeping ducks and hens.

His intention is to sell their eggs. You need to calculate the dimensions of his paddock, work out how many ducks and hens he can buy, and calculate the price of his duck eggs.

Fencing the paddock

A farmer wants to fence three sides of a rectangular paddock. One side already has a fence.

- Call the lengths of the sides of the paddock x and y.
- The area of the paddock must be 6000 m^2.
- He uses 230 m of fencing.

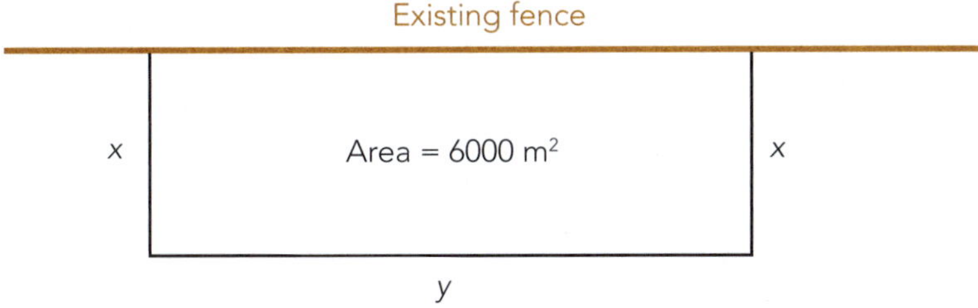

By using all the available fencing, find possible dimensions for his paddock so that it has an area of 6000 m^2.

Buying ducks and hens

He needs to buy ducks and hens to live in his paddock.

- Ducks cost $30 each and hens cost $20 each.
- He has budgeted $680 to spend on the ducks and hens.
- The relationship between the number of ducks and the number of hens that he buys is given by $x^2 + 4y = 208$, where x represents the number of ducks and y represents the number of hens.

How many ducks and hens did he buy?

Selling eggs

The farmer is going to sell duck eggs and hens' eggs to pay for the fencing.

- He can sell his hens' eggs for \$0.50 each.
- He wants to earn \$16 per day from the sale of all his eggs.
- The relationship between the average number of duck eggs and the average number of hens' eggs that he gets each day is modelled by $y + 22x = x^2 + 132$, where x represents the daily average number of duck eggs and y represents the daily average number of hens' eggs.
- There needs to be only one possibility for the average number of duck eggs and the average number of hens' eggs that he gets each day.
- He needs to know the price to put on his duck eggs, and the average number of each type of egg that he will need each day.

ISBN: 9780170416009

Answers

Straight lines (pp. 5–16)

The gradient of a line (pp. 5–7)

1 **a** $m = 1$ **b** $m = \frac{3}{2} = 1.5$
c $m = \frac{2}{6} = 0.\dot{3}$ **d** $m = 0$
e $m = -\frac{4}{3} = 1.\dot{3}$ **f** $m = -\frac{5}{2} = -2.5$
g $m = \frac{4}{5} = 0.8$ **h** undefined
i $m = \frac{2}{4} = 0.5$ **j** $m = -\frac{1}{8} = -0.125$

2

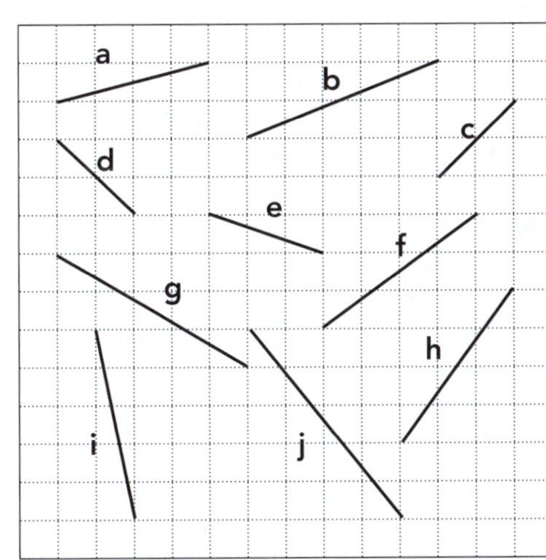

Finding the equation of a straight line (pp. 8–15)

1 Using the gradient and the *y*-intercept (pp. 8–9)

1

Line	m	c	y = mx + c
———	2	3	$y = 2x + 3$
------	−3	−2	$y = -3x - 2$
- - - -	$\frac{3}{4}$	0	$y = \frac{3}{4}x$
- — -	$\frac{3}{5}$	−5	$y = \frac{3}{5}x - 5$
———	$-\frac{1}{5}$	3	$y = -\frac{1}{5}x + 3$
———	$-\frac{2}{3}$	−4	$y = -\frac{2}{3}x - 4$

2 $y = -2x + 5$ **3** $y = 1.5x - 3$
4 $y = 2.5$ **5** $y = 7x + 4$
6 $y = -\frac{1}{3}x$ **7** $y = \frac{4}{3}x + 5$
8 $y = px - 3$ **9** $y = -\frac{2}{5}x + q$

2 Using the gradient and one point (pp. 10–11)

1 $y = 5x - 11$ **2** $y = 3x + 7$
3 $y = \frac{1}{2}x - 7$ **4** $y = -x + 9$
5 $y = -2$ **6** $y = -\frac{1}{2}x - 3$
7 $y = \frac{3}{4}x - 9$ **8** $y = -\frac{5}{8}x - \frac{1}{8}$
9 $y = 2x - 7$ **10** $y = -\frac{2}{3}x + 8$
11 $y = \frac{5}{4}x - 14\frac{3}{4}$ **12** $y = -\frac{4}{3}x + 9$
13 $y = \frac{9}{4}x$

3 Using two points (pp. 12–13)

1 $y = 3x + 7$ **2** $y = 5x - 2$
3 $y = \frac{1}{2}x + 4$ **4** $y = \frac{3}{4}x - 3$
5 $y = -2x + 5$ **6** $y = -x - 7$
7 $y = -\frac{1}{8}x + 3$ **8** $y = \frac{2}{3}x - 4$
9 $y = \frac{5}{3}x + 12$ **10** $y = -\frac{3}{4}x + 10$
11 $y = -\frac{3}{8}x - 5$ **12** $y = -\frac{3}{5}x - 16$

4 From practical information (pp. 14–15)

1 **a** $x + y = 258$ **b** $5x + 12y = 2418$
c $x - y = 17$ **d** $x = 3y$
e $x + 5 = 2y$ **f** $12y - 5x = 1781$
2 **a** $2x + 2y = 84$ **b** $x - y = 6$
c $x = 2y - 1$
d $P = 2y + x$ and $P = x + 2y$

Putting it all together (p. 16)

1 **a** **i** $y = 2$ **ii** $x = 5$
b $y = x + 3$ **c** $y = -x + 13$
d $y = -2x + 11$
2 **a** $y = \frac{3}{4}x + 1$ **b** $y = -\frac{4}{3}x + 17\frac{2}{3}$
c $y = \frac{4}{3}x + 4\frac{2}{3}$

ISBN: 9780170416009

Recognising graphs of curves (pp. 17–36)

Parabolas — matching equations with graphs (pp. 21–23)

1 a C b D
c B d A
2 a D b B
c A d C
3 a A b G
c F d H
e E f B
g C h D
4 a F b D
c C d E
e B f A

Circles — matching equations with graphs (pp. 27–28)

1 a A b H
c F d G
e D f C
g B h E
2 a D b C
c A d B
3 a C b B
c D d A

Hyperbolas — matching equations with graphs (pp. 33–34)

1 a D b A
c C d B
2 a D b C
c B d A
3 a C b A
c B d D
4 a B b D
c A d C

Mixing it up (pp. 35–36)

1 a E b C
c A d G
e H f F
g D h B
2 a E b G
c H d C
e B f A
g F h D

Quadratic expressions (pp. 37–51)

Expanding (pp. 37–38)

1 $x^2 + 5x + 6$ 2 $x^2 + 3x - 10$
3 $x^2 + 11x + 28$ 4 $x^2 + 18x + 81$
5 $3x^2 + x - 2$ 6 $8x^2 + 14x - 15$
7 $9x^2 - 24x + 16$ 8 $x^2 - 10x + 25$
9 $-2x^2 - x + 3$ 10 $-4x^2 - 7x + 15$
11 $18x^2 + 21x - 15$ 12 $-21x^2 + 65x + 44$
13 $x^2 - 9$ 14 $16x^2 - 49$
15 $-4x^2 + 25$ 16 $100x^2 + 100x + 25$

Factorising quadratics (pp. 39–43)

1 Where the coefficient of x^2 is 1 (pp. 39–40)

1 $(x + 2)(x + 5)$ 2 $(x + 3)(x + 12)$
3 $(x + 1)(x + 9)$ 4 $(x + 6)(x - 2)$
5 $(x + 6)(x + 8)$ 6 $(x - 7)(x - 3)$
7 $(x - 8)(x + 3)$ 8 $(6 + x)(4 + x)$
9 $(x + 7)(x - 7)$ 10 $(1 + x)(1 - x)$
11 $(x - 6)^2$ 12 $(5 + x)(5 - x)$
13 $(3 + 2y)(3 - 2y)$
14 $(10 + x)(10 - x)$ or $-(x + 10)(x - 10)$
15 $-(x + 2)(x + 3)$
16 $(x + 6)(1 - x)$ or $-(x + 6)(x - 1)$
17 $(x - 4)(2 - x)$ or $(x - 2)(4 - x)$ or $-(x - 2)(x - 4)$
18 $(6 - 4x)(6 + 4x)$

2 Where the coefficient of x^2 is not 1, but there is a common factor (p. 41)

1 $3(x + 5)(x - 2)$ 2 $2(x + 7)(x - 7)$
3 $-4(x + 1)(x - 1)$ 4 $8(5 + x)(5 - x)$
5 $-5(x + 1)^2$ 6 $-4(x + 1)(x + 3)$
7 $2(x - 3)(x + 2)$ 8 $5(x + 6)(x - 6)$

3 Where the coefficient of x^2 is not 1 and there is no common factor (pp. 42–43)

1 $(3x + 2)(x + 5)$ 2 $(2x + 3)(x + 4)$
3 $(5x + 2)(3x + 1)$ 4 $(x + 5)(3x - 1)$
5 $(4x + 1)(x - 7)$ 6 $(x - 3)(5x - 1)$
7 $(2x - 9)(2x + 1)$ 8 $(3x + 1)(2x - 5)$
9 $(5x + 2)(4x - 3)$
10 $(7x - 2)(3x - 5)$
11 $(2x + 3)(2 - x)$ or $-(2x + 3)(x - 2)$
12 $(5x - 1)(4 - x)$ or $-(5x - 1)(x - 4)$ or $(1 - 5x)(x - 4)$
13 $(2x + 5)(7 - 3x)$ or $-(2x + 5)(3x - 7)$
14 $(2x - 5)(2x + 5)$
15 $(6x - 7)(6x + 7)$
16 $(2x + 9)^2$
17 $(3x - 5)^2$
18 $(7x + 4)(2 - 5x)$ or $-(7x + 4)(5x - 2)$

Solving quadratic equations (pp. 44–48)

1 By factorising (pp. 44–45)

1 $x = -2$ or -4 2 $x = 2$ or 5
3 $x = 7$ or -3 4 $x = 0$ or 6
5 $x = 3$ or -4 6 $x = \pm 7$
7 $x = \pm 2.5$ 8 $x = 7$ or -3
9 $x = -1$ or -1.5 10 $x = 0.2$ or -1.5
11 $x = 0.25$ or -3 12 $x = 0.75$ or 0.4

ISBN: 9780170416009

2 Using the quadratic formula (pp. 46–47)

1 $x = -2$ or -4
2 $x = 2$ or 5
3 $x = 7$ or -3
4 $x = 0$ or 6
5 $x = 3$ or -4
6 $x = \pm 7$
7 $x = 2.6$ or -1
8 $x = 1.147$ or -2.397
9 $x = 6.854$ or 0.1459
10 $x = 3.076$ or -1.409
11 $x = 5.303$ or 1.697
12 $x = 6.372$ or 0.628

3 On a calculator (p. 48)

1 $x = -2$ or -4
2 $x = 2$ or 5
3 $x = 7$ or -3
4 $x = 0$ or 6
5 $x = 3$ or -4
6 $x = \pm 7$
7 $x = 2.\dot{6}$ or -1
8 $x = 1.147$ or -2.397
9 $x = 6.854$ or 0.1458
10 $x = 3.076$ or -1.408
11 $x = 5.303$ or 1.697
12 $x = 6.372$ or 0.628

Finding how many solutions exist (pp. 49–51)

1 $\Delta = 81 \therefore$ 2 roots
2 $\Delta = 0 \therefore$ 1 root
3 $\Delta = -7 \therefore$ 0 roots
4 $\Delta = 3 \therefore$ 2 roots
5 $\Delta = 9 \therefore$ 2 roots
6 $\Delta = -31 \therefore$ 0 roots
7 $\Delta = 0 \therefore$ 1 root
8 $\Delta = 0 \therefore$ 1 root
9 $\Delta = -8 \therefore$ 0 roots
10 $\Delta = 97 \therefore$ 2 roots
11 $\Delta = -11 \therefore$ 0 roots
12 $\Delta = -1 \therefore$ 0 roots
13 $\Delta = 409 \therefore$ 2 roots
14 $\Delta = 49 \therefore$ 2 roots
15 $\Delta = 0 \therefore$ 1 root
16 $\Delta = -100 \therefore$ 0 roots
17 $\Delta = 0 \therefore$ 1 root
18 $\Delta = 4620 \therefore$ 2 roots

Simultaneous equations (pp. 52–77)

Line and parabola (pp. 52–55)

1 Solve $x^2 + x - 2 = 0$
$\Delta = 9 \therefore$ 2 roots
Solutions: (1, 3) and (–2, 6)

2 Solve $x^2 + 2x + 1 = 0$
$\Delta = 0 \therefore$ 1 root
Solution: (–1, 1)

3 Solve $x^2 - x - 6 = 0$
$\Delta = 25 \therefore$ 2 roots
Solutions: (–2, –4) and (3, 6)

4 Solve $x^2 - 2.5x + 3 = 0$
$\Delta = -5.75 \therefore$ 0 roots

5 Solve $x^2 - 6x + 5 = 0$
$\Delta = 16 \therefore$ 2 roots
Solutions: (1, 0) and (5, –8)

6 Solve $x^2 + 2x + 1 = 0$
$\Delta = 0 \therefore$ 1 root
Solution: (–1, –5)

7 Solve $x^2 - 11x - 31 = 0$
$\Delta = -3 \therefore$ 0 roots

8 Solve $x^2 - 16 = 0$
$\Delta = 64 \therefore$ 2 roots
Solutions: (–4, –3) and (4, 21)

9 Solve $x^2 - 1x + 11 = 0$
$\Delta = 100 \therefore$ 2 roots
Solutions: (1, 52) and (11, 22)

10 Solve $x^2 - 21x + 90 = 0$
$\Delta = 81 \therefore$ 2 roots
Solutions: (6, 51) and (15, 15)

11 Solve $x^2 - 6x + 9 = 0$
$\Delta = 0 \therefore$ 1 root
Solution: (3, 61)

12 Solve $x^2 - 28x + 196 = 0$
$\Delta = 0 \therefore$ 1 root
Solution: (14, 195)

Line and circle (pp. 56–59)

1 Solve $x^2 - x - 12 = 0$
$\Delta = 49 \therefore$ 2 roots
Solutions: (–3, –4) and (4, 3)

2 Solve $x^2 - 7x + 10 = 0$
$\Delta = 9 \therefore$ 2 roots
Solutions: (5, –2) and (2, –5)

3 Solve $x^2 - 6x - 7 = 0$
$\Delta = 64 \therefore$ 2 roots
Solutions: (7, –1) and (–1, 7)

4 Solve $x^2 - 12x + 36 = 0$
$\Delta = 0 \therefore$ 1 root
Solution: (6, 6)

5 Solve $2x^2 - 20x + 55 = 0$
$\Delta = -40 \therefore$ 0 roots

6 Solve $x^2 - 25 = 0$
$\Delta = 100 \therefore$ 2 roots
Solutions: (–5, 6) and (5, 6)

7 Solve $5x^2 + 45x + 104 = 0$
$\Delta = -55 \therefore$ 0 roots

8 Solve $x^2 - 25 = 0$
$\Delta = 100 \therefore$ 2 roots
Solutions: (–5, –5) and (5, 3)

9 Solve $x^2 - 7x - 44 = 0$
$\Delta = 225 \therefore$ 2 roots
Solutions: (–4, 9) and (11, –6)

10 Solve $x^2 - 144 = 0$
$\Delta = 576 \therefore$ 2 roots
Solutions: (–12, 5) and 12, –5)

11 Solve $5x^2 + 160x + 1294 = 0$
$\Delta = -280 \therefore$ 0 roots

12 Solve $x^2 - 14x - 49 = 0$
$\Delta = 0 \therefore$ 1 root
Solution: (7, 4)

Line and hyperbola (pp. 60–63)

1 Solve $x^2 - 16 = 0$
$\Delta = 64 \therefore$ 2 roots
Solutions: (–4, –4) and (4, 4)

2 Solve $x^2 + 4x - 12 = 0$
$\Delta = 64 \therefore$ 2 roots
Solutions: (–6, –2) and (2, 6)

3 Solve $x^2 + 10x - 25 = 0$
$\Delta = 0 \therefore$ 1 root
Solution: (–5, 5)

4 Solve $x^2 - 9 = 0$
$\Delta = 36 \therefore$ 2 roots
Solutions: (–3, –12) and (3, 12)

5 Solve $x^2 + 4x + 5 = 0$
$\Delta = -4 \therefore$ 0 roots

6 Solve $x^2 - x - 6 = 0$
$\Delta = 25 \therefore$ 2 roots
Solutions: (–2, 2) and (3, 7)

7 Solve $x^2 + 5x + 4 = 0$
$\Delta = 9 \therefore$ 2 roots
Solutions: (–4, –10) and (–1, 5)

8 Solve $x^2 - 6x + 9 = 0$
$\Delta = 0 \therefore$ 1 root
Solution: (3, 10)

9 Solve $2x^2 - 45x + 256 = 0$
$\Delta = -23 \therefore$ 0 roots

10 Solve $x^2 - 16x + 48 = 0$
$\Delta = 144 \therefore$ 2 roots
Solutions: (4, 0) and (12, 12)

11 Solve $x^2 + 6x + 9 = 0$
$\Delta = 0 \therefore$ 1 root
Solution: (–3, 6)

12 It is easier to simplify in terms of y.
Solve $y^2 - 22y + 112 = 0$
$\Delta = 36 \therefore$ 2 roots
Solutions: (31, 14) and (13, 8)

Finding unknown values, given the number of solutions (pp. 64–67)

1 a $p = \pm 14$
b (–7, –7) and (7, 7)
c $p^2 - px + 49 = 0$
No solutions $\Rightarrow$ $b^2 - 4ac < 0$
$p^2 - 4 \times 1 \times 49 < 0$
$p^2 - 196 < 0$
$p < 14$ or $p > -14$

2 a $p = 50$
b (5, 5)
c $x^2 + y^2 = 50$ forms a circle and $y = 10 - x$ forms a tangent to it. They meet at (5, 5).
d $2x^2 - 20x + (100 - p) = 0$
2 solutions $\Rightarrow$ $b^2 - 4ac > 0$
$400 - 4 \times 2 \times (100 - p) > 0$
$400 - 800 + 8p > 0$
$8p > 400$
$p > 50$

3 a $p = -13$
b (4, 3)
c $y = x^2 - 8x + (29 + p)$
2 solutions $\Rightarrow$ $b^2 - 4ac > 0$
$64 - 4 \times 1 \times (29 + p) > 0$
$64 - 116 - 4p > 0$
$-4p > 52$
$p < -13$

4 a $p = 0.5$ or -5.5
b (3, –1) and (–3, 14)
c The lines $y = 0.5x - 2.5$ and $y = -5.5x - 2.5$ form tangents to the parabola $y = 0.5(x - 1)(x - 4)$
d $0.5x^2 - (p + 2.5)x + 4.5 = 0$
No solutions $\Rightarrow$ $b^2 - 4ac < 0$
$(p + 2.5)^2 - 4 \times 0.5 \times 4.5 < 0$
$p^2 + 5p + 6.25 - 9 < 0$
$p^2 + 5p - 2.75 < 0$
$(p + 0.5)(p - 5.5) < 0$
$-5.5 < p < 0.5$

Mixing it up, with applications (pp. 68–77)

1 a

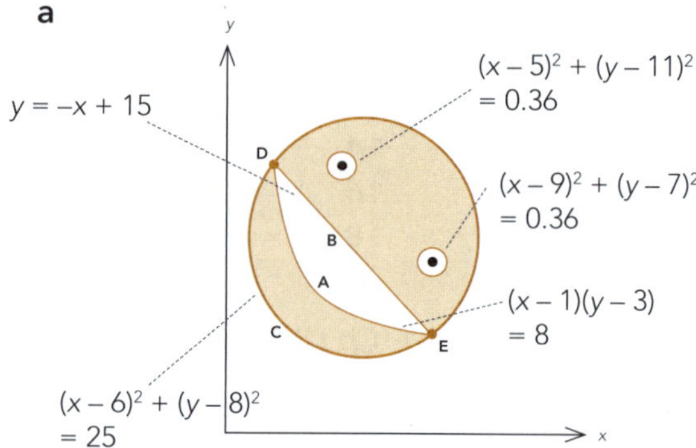

b (2, 11) and (9, 4)
c (2, 11) and (9, 4)

2 a

Will:	$15
Sefa:	$30
Jack:	$35

b

Will:	$0
Sefa:	$20
Jack:	$10

$\therefore$ Sefa has the most.
c $5 per day, because the gradient of the line is –5.
d On day seven they both had $25 left.
e Equation must pass through (10, 20)
$\therefore$ Equation is $y = 60 - 4x$

3 a $y = 130 - 10x$
b Both baches cost the friends $90 each per night if four of them go, or $40 each per night if nine of them go.
c If fewer than four go, then Ben's Bach is cheaper.
If four go, they both cost the same.
If five, six, seven or eight of them go, then Cosy Cottage is cheaper.

ISBN: 9780170416009

If nine go, they both cost the same.
If 10, 11 or 12 go, then Ben's Bach is cheaper.

d The cost of hiring the baches is the same ($60 per night) if six people go for the weekend.
Otherwise Ben's Bach is always cheaper.

4 a Equation of AB is $(x - 5)^2 + (y - 34)^2 = 25$ because this is the only equation of the form $x^2 \ldots\ldots + y^2 \ldots\ldots = \ldots\ldots$ (i.e. circle equation).

b Coordinates of A are (0, 34) and coordinates of B are (5, 29) because:

- the $(y - 34)$ in the circle equation means that the centre of the circle is at $y = 34$
- the $(x - 5)$ means that the centre of the circle is at $x = 5$
- the '25' means that the diameter of the circle is 5.

c Coordinates of B are (5, 29) and coordinates of C are (25, 25).

$\therefore m = \frac{25 - 29}{25 - 5} = -\frac{4}{20} = -\frac{1}{5}$

Equation of BC is $(y - y_1) = m(x - x_1)$

$$y - 29 = -\frac{1}{5}(x - 5)$$
$$y = -\frac{1}{5}x + 30$$

d Equation of DE is $y = \frac{1}{2}(x - 21) + 10$ because it is the only equation which expands to $y = ax^2 \ldots\ldots$

e $x = 26$ and $y = \frac{1}{2}(x - 21)^2 + 10 \Rightarrow y = 22.5$

$\therefore$ The coordinates of D are (26, 22.5).

f Coordinates of C are (25, 25) and coordinates of D are (26, 22.5).

$\therefore m = \frac{25 - 22.5}{25 - 26} = -2.5$ or $-\frac{5}{2}$

Equation of CD is $(y - y_1) = m(x - x_1)$

$$y - 25 = -\frac{5}{2}(x - 25)$$
$$y = -\frac{5}{2}x + 87.5$$

g E is where $y = 2x + c$ is a tangent to $y = \frac{1}{2}(x - 21)^2 + 10 \Rightarrow b^2 - 4ac = 0$

$\therefore$ Solve $y = \frac{1}{2}(x - 21)^2 + 10$ and $y = 2x + c$

$$\Rightarrow x^2 - 46x + (461 - 2c) = 0$$

$b^2 - 4ac = 0 \Rightarrow c = -34$

$\therefore$ Equation of EF is $y = 2x - 34$

h Equation of FG is $(x - 22)y = -12$ because this is the only equation that would expand to $y = xy \ldots\ldots$

i F is where $(x - 22)y = -12$ and $y = 2x - 34$ meet.

$\therefore$ Solve $(x - 22)y = -12$ and $y = 2x - 34$

$\Rightarrow x = 19$ or 20

$\therefore$ Possible locations for F are (19, 4) and (20, 6).

5 a Solutions are (10, 0) and (18, 16)

b $y = \frac{1}{3}x + 10$ **c** $y = -\frac{3}{4}x + 5$

6 a

Aroha:	22.5 cm
Brody:	28 cm
Clara:	22.5 cm

b Both Aroha and Clara, whose sunflowers were both 60 cm high. Brody's was 52 cm high.

$\therefore$ Aroha and Clara won by 8 cm.

c Need to solve $x^2 - 75x = 0$.
After 75 days; and the sunflowers were 50 cm high.

d $y = \frac{1}{2}x + 20$

7 a (3, 6)

b $y = -2x + 12$

c $y = 2x - 8$

d $x^2 - 14x + (2p + 9) = 0$

Two solutions $\Rightarrow b^2 - 4ac = 0$

$$196 - 4 \times 1 \times (2p + 9) = 0$$
$$196 - 8p - 36 = 0$$
$$8p = 160$$
$$p = 20$$

$\therefore$ Equation of BD is $y = -2x + 20$

8 a (5, 8) and (10, 9)

b $y = 8.4$ meets the ceiling at (7, 8.4).
$y = 8.4$ meets the wall where $8.4 = -0.2(x - 1)(x - 15) \Rightarrow x = 5.354$ or 10.646.
(5.354, 8.4) is on the left wall of the tunnel, so above the ceiling.
(10.646, 8.4) is on the right wall of the tunnel.
Width of tunnel where $y = 8.4$ is $10.646 - 7 = 3.646$.
$\therefore$ Piece of machinery will fit, but with only 0.146 m to spare.

c One solution to $x^2 - 22x + (15 + 5p) = 0 \Rightarrow b^2 - 4ac = 0$

$\therefore p = 21.2$

(brace equation $y = -1.2x + 21.2$)

ISBN: 9780170416009

Practice tasks (pp. 78–84)

Practice task one (pp. 78–80)

Year 9 welcome day

Sold 350 items ⇒ $x + y = 340$, so $y = 350 - x$

Equations to be solved:

$y = 350 - x$ and $x^2 + 2y = 25\,980$

$\therefore x^2 - 2x - 25\,280 = 0$

Solutions: $x = 160$ or -158

Cannot sell a negative number of melon slices, so they sold 160 melon slices.

∴ Number of Juicies sold = 350 – 160 = 190.

They charged \$0.50 for melon slices and the total money was \$270

⇒ $160 \times 0.50 + 190j = 270$, where j represents the price of Juicies.

$\therefore j = \$1.00$

They sold 160 melon slices at \$0.50 each, and 190 Juicies at \$1 each.

The gala sports day

They sold melon slices for \$0.50 and Juicies for \$0.90, and after all the melon slices and Juicies were sold, they had \$102

⇒ $0.5x + 0.9y = 102$

$\therefore x = 204 - 1.8y$

Equations to be solved:

$x = 204 - 1.8y$ and $3xy + 10x = 15\,000$

$\therefore y^2 - 110y + 2400 = 0$

Solutions: $y = 80$ or 30

$y = 80 \Rightarrow x = 60$, so they could have sold 60 melon slices and 80 Juicies ⇒ total items = 140

or $y = 30 \Rightarrow x = 150$, so they could have sold 150 melon slices and 30 Juicies ⇒ total items = 180.

They sold fewer than 150 items, so they sold 60 melon slices at \$0.50 each and 80 Juicies at \$0.90 each.

The swimming sports

They charged \$1 each for Juicies, and let the price for melon slices be m.

⇒ $mx + y = 109$, so $y = 109 - mx$

Equations to be solved:

$y = 109 - mx$ and $100y = 10\,000 - x^2$

$\therefore x^2 - 100mx + 900 = 0$

One solution → $b^2 - 4ac = 0$

⇒ $(-100m)^2 - 4 \times 1 \times 900 = 0$

⇒ $m = 0.6$, so they charge \$0.60 for melon slices.

$\therefore y = 109 - 0.6x$

To find the number of melon slices sold, solve $x^2 - 100(0.6)x + 900 = 0$:

⇒ $x = 30$

$\therefore y = 109 - 0.6(30) = 91$.

They sold 30 melon slices at \$0.60 each and 91 Juicies at \$1.00 each.

Practice task two (pp. 81–82)

The black dot

Equations to be solved:

$y + x^2 + 34 = 16x$ and $y = 4x - 34$

$y = 4x - 34$ was selected because the lower y-intercept (–34) means that $y = 4x - 34$ must be to the right of $y = 4x - 16$.

$\therefore x^2 - 12x = 0$ or $x(x - 12) = 0$

Solutions: $x = 0$ or $x = 12$.

∴ Possible coordinates for the black dot are (0, –34) and (12, 14).

The diagonal line must cut the entire parabola in two places: one would be below and to the left of the logo, and the other at the black dot. (0, –34) is lower and further to the left than (12, 14).

∴ The black dot is at (12, 14).

The gold dot

Equations to be solved:

$(x - 8)^2 + y^2 = 25$ and $y = 4x - 16$

$\therefore 17x^2 - 144x + 295 = 0$

Solutions: $x = 5$ or $x = 3.471$.

∴ Possible coordinates for the black dot are (5, 4) and (3.471, –2.116).

The diagonal line must cut the entire circle in two places: one would be below and to the left of the logo, and the other at the red dot. (3.471, –2.116) is lower and further to the left than (5, 4).

∴ The gold dot is at (5, 4).

The equation of this new line, and the point at which it touches the parabola

1 To find the equation of the tangent:

To be parallel with the other diagonal lines, it must have the equation $y = 4x + c$.

To find values for c:

Solve $y = 4x - c$ and $y + x^2 + 34 = 16x$

⇒ $x^2 - 12x + (34 + c) = 0$

One solution → $b^2 - 4ac = 0$

⇒ $(-12)^2 - 4 \times 1 \times (34 + c) = 0$

⇒ $c = 2$

∴ Equation is $y = 4x + 2$

 ISBN: 9780170416009

2 To find the point where the tangent touches the parabola:
Equations to be solved:
$y + x^2 + 34 = 16x$ and $y = 4x + 2$
$\therefore x^2 - 12x + 36 = 0$
Solution: $x = 6$
$\therefore$ Point where the line touches the parabola is (6, 26).

Practice task three (pp. 83–84)

Fencing the paddock

Equations to be solved:
Length of fencing required: $2x + y = 230$ or $y = -2x + 230$
Area of paddock: $xy = 6000$
$\therefore 2x^2 - 230x + 6000 = 0$
Solutions: $x = 40$ or $x = 75$.
The paddock can be either 40 m by 150 m or 75 m by 80 m.

Buying ducks and hens

Equations to be solved:
Cost of ducks and hens: $30x + 20y = 680$
Relationship between them: $x^2 + 4y = 208$
$\therefore x^2 - 6x - 72 = 0$
Solutions: $x = -6$ or $x = 12$.
The solution cannot be negative (for the number of ducks).
He buys 12 ducks and 16 hens.

Selling eggs

Let p be the price of a duck egg
$\Rightarrow px + 0.5y = 16$
To find values for p:
Solve $y = 32 - px$ and $y + 22x = x^2 + 132$
$\Rightarrow x^2 + x(2p - 22) + 100 = 0$
One solution $\rightarrow b^2 - 4ac = 0$
$\Rightarrow (2p - 22)^2 - 4 \times 1 \times 100 = 0$
$\therefore p^2 - 22p + 21 = 0$
Solutions: $p = 1$ or $p = 21$
$p = 1$
Solve $y = 32 - 2x$ and $y + 22x = x^2 + 132$
$\Rightarrow x^2 - 20x + 100 = 0$
Solutions: $x = 10$, so $y = 12$
$p = 21$
Solve $y = 32 - 42x$ and $y + 22x = x^2 + 132$
$\Rightarrow x^2 + 20x + 100 = 0$
Solution: $x = -10$. Not possible to average a negative number of eggs.

$\therefore$ In order to earn \$16 per day, he should sell his duck eggs for \$1 each, and he needs to produce an average of 10 duck eggs and 12 hens' eggs per day.

ISBN: 9780170416009